MW00960931

BRYAN CAPLAN

Labor Econ Versus the World

Essays on the World's Greatest Market

Edited by Jack Pfefferkorn
Cover art by @sengsavanedesign

Copyright © 2021 by Bryan Caplan

All rights reserved. No part of this publication may be reproduced, stored or transmitted in any form or by any means, electronic, mechanical, photocopying, recording, scanning, or otherwise without written permission from the publisher. It is illegal to copy this book, post it to a website, or distribute it by any other means without permission.

First edition

Published by Bet On It Books

Fairfax, VA 22030

To Steve Kuhn, who taught me to dream bigger.

Contents

II Open Borders

III Education Without Romance

Part I

Laissez-Faire and Labor

Labor Econ Versus the World

My 13-year-old homeschooled sons just finished my labor economics class.[1] I hope they take many more economics classes, but I'll be perfectly satisfied with their grasp of economics as long as they internalize what they learned this semester. Why? Because a *good* labor economics class contains everything you need to see through the central tenets of our society's secular religion. Labor economics stands against the world. Once you grasp its lessons, you can never again be a normal citizen.

What are these "central tenets of our secular religion" and what's wrong with them?

Tenet #1: The main reason today's workers have a decent standard of living is that government passed a bunch of laws protecting them.

Critique: High worker productivity plus competition between employers is the real reason today's workers have a decent standard of living. In fact, "pro-worker" laws have dire negative side effects for workers, especially unemployment.

Tenet #2: Strict regulation of immigration, especially low-skilled immigration, prevents poverty and inequality.

Critique: Immigration restrictions massively *increase* the poverty and inequality of the world – and make the average American poorer in the process. Specialization and trade are fountains of wealth, and immigration is just specialization and trade in labor.

Tenet #3: In the modern economy, nothing is more important than education.

Critique: After making obvious corrections for pre-existing ability, completion probability, and such, the return to education is pretty good for strong students, but mediocre or worse for weak students.

Tenet #4: The modern welfare state strikes a wise balance between compassion and efficiency.

Critique: The welfare state primarily helps the old, not the poor – and 19th-century open immigration did far more for the *absolutely* poor than the welfare state ever has.

Tenet #5: Increasing education levels is good for society.

Critique: Education is mostly signaling; increasing education is a recipe for credential inflation, not prosperity.

Tenet #6: Racial and gender discrimination remains a serious problem, and without government regulation, would still be rampant.

Critique: Unless government *requires* discrimination, market forces make it a marginal issue at most. Large group differences persist because groups differ largely in productivity.

Tenet #7: Men have treated women poorly throughout history, and it's only thanks to feminism that anything's improved.

Critique: While women in the pre-modern era lived hard lives, so did men. The mating market led to poor outcomes for women because men had very little to offer. Economic growth plus competition in labor and mating markets, not

4

feminism, is the main reason women's lives improved.

Tenet #8: Overpopulation is a terrible social problem.

Critique: The positive externalities of population – especially idea externalities – far outweigh the negative. Reducing population to help the environment is using a sword to kill a mosquito.

Yes, I'm well aware that most labor economics classes either neglect these points or strive for "balance." But as far as I'm concerned, most labor economists just aren't doing their job. Their lingering faith in our society's secular religion clouds their judgment – and prevents them from enlightening their students and laying the groundwork for a better future.

December 21, 2015

* * *

Notes

1. Caplan, Bryan. "Why I'm Homeschooling." *EconLog*, September 22, 2015.

Labor Econ Versus the World: Further Thoughts

1. In my youth, I saw Industrial Organization as the heart of our secular religion. My history textbooks loudly and repeatedly decried "monopoly"; teachers, peers, and parents echoed their complaints. Since the late-90s, however, such complaints have faded from public discourse. The reason isn't that plausible examples of monopolies have vanished. If anything, firms that look like monopolies – Amazon, Costco, Walmart, Starbucks, Uber, Facebook, Twitter – are higher-profile than ever. But the insight I preached in my youth – the main way firms obtain and hold monopoly on the free market is reliably giving consumers great deals – is almost conventional wisdom. What modern consumer fears Amazon or Starbucks?

2. Another reason Industrial Organization has faded from our secular religion: Thanks to e-commerce and internet reviews, it's now indisputable that reputation impels firms to treat their customers well. When people want to buy with confidence, almost no one asks, "Does the government regulate this?" Instead, they scrutinize the seller's reputation.

3. Since moderns are satisfied with markets as consumers, it's only natural that our secular religion focuses on *producers*.

For the vast majority of us, "producer" means "employee."

4. The main lesson of labor econ is that markets for labor closely resemble markets for other goods. Why then are people so eager to believe that unregulated labor markets are terrible? Part of the reason is that the little differences are occasionally traumatic. Wages *don't* adjust like stock market prices, so involuntary unemployment is a real and frightening prospect.[1]

5. Another important reason, though, is that markets where people trade vaguely-defined products for cash tend to be acrimonious. When products are vague, the side paying cash often feels ripped off, and the side receiving cash often feels insulted. In most markets, sellers strive to standardize products to preempt this acrimony. In labor markets, however, this is inherently difficult because every human is unique. As a result, employers often lash out at workers because they feel cheated, and employees often resent employers because they feel mistreated.[2]

6. These problems are amplified by the fact that our jobs are central to our identities. So when we feel mistreated by a boss (or by co-workers the boss fails to control), we experience it as a serious affront. This in turn leads people to demonize employers as a class.

7. Once you demonize employers, it's natural to (a) look to government for salvation from current ills, and (b) imagine that existing "pro-labor" laws explain why the demons in our lives don't already treat us far worse. This isn't just the root of our secular religion. If you take the demonization of employers and salvation by government literally, you end up with Marxism or something like it.

December 22, 2015

7

* * *

Notes

1. Caplan, Bryan. "The Grave Evil of Unemployment." *EconLog*, April 23, 2013.
2. Caplan, Bryan. "Scott Alexander on Labor Economics: Point-by-Point Reply." *EconLog*, September 2, 2015.

Labor Econ Versus the World:
Ecumenical Edition

M ost courses in labor economics *don't* strive to undermine our society's secular religion.[1] Mine does. I suspect that most labor econ professors would object to my efforts. Shouldn't a college class provide a balanced discussion of the issues, instead of trying to change the way students see the world?

Yes and no. Of course, college classes should provide a balanced discussion of the issues. But if students arrive with a bunch of silly preconceptions, changing the way students see the world is a *precondition* for balanced discussion. Take evolution. Of course, a good class in evolution provides a balanced discussion of the issues. But if students arrive as committed creationists, the professor can't teach them until creationism has been thoroughly critiqued.

But are there really any popular preconceptions in labor economics as ludicrous as creationism? I say there are, starting with what I called Tenet #1 of our secular religion: "The main reason today's workers have a decent standard of living is that government passed a bunch of laws protecting them." How do we know it's false? Most obviously, because even if you assume *zero* disincentive effects, *equally* dividing premodern incomes still yields absolute poverty. More subtly, because employers treat *most* workers far better than the law requires; competition's the only credible explanation. How do we know Tenet #1 is popular? Because it's ubiquitous; until you study economics, it's virtually the *only* story you hear.

I'm well-aware that many – perhaps most – labor economists – consider labor regulation on balance helpful for workers. Not critical, just helpful. Even if they're right, they should still spend ample time dissecting Tenet #1. Why? Because you can't have a reasonable discussion of the costs and benefits of labor regulation until you root out all the silly hyperbole students bring to the table.[2]

Think about how few successful politicians of either party openly favor the abolition of the minimum wage. A few support the minimum wage because they're convinced labor demand is highly inelastic. All the rest just rely on our secular religion: passing "pro-worker" laws is a clear-cut way to dramatically help the common man.

My fellow labor economists' mistake: Since they weigh the merits of labor regulation for a living, they forget that non-economists can't even imagine what the downsides might be. If professors fail to spell them out in gory detail, students will remain oblivious to the downsides for the rest of their lives.

December 23, 2015

* * *

Notes

1. Caplan, Bryan. "Labor Econ Versus the World." *EconLog,*

December 21, 2015.

2. Caplan, Bryan. "What's Libertarian About Betting?" *EconLog*, September 30, 2015.

The Anti-Jerk Law

You've probably had a boss who was a jerk. Indeed, you may be working under a jerk of a boss right now. Question: Would it be a good idea to pass an Anti-Jerk Law to protect workers from these jerky employers? Like existing employment discrimination laws, the Anti-Jerk Law would allow aggrieved employees to sue their employer for jerkiness – and receive handsome compensation if they prove their charge in a court of law.

I doubt many people would endorse this Anti-Jerk Law. On what basis, though, would they object?

Libertarians might stand up for the "right to be a jerk," but few non-libertarians would find that convincing.

Economists might appeal to the standard economics text-book conclusion that mandated benefits – including the right to sue your employer for jerkiness – are inefficient. But few non-economists would find *that* convincing.

Why, then, would *normal* people refuse to endorse an Anti-Jerk Law?[1] If pressed, the reason would probably be along the lines of, "Jerkiness is way too subjective." If you call your boss a jerk, he's probably thinking, "No, *you're* the jerk." Even if a large majority of the workers at a firm consider their boss a jerk, a contrarian might insist, "The boss is tough but fair. You folks simply don't measure up." Other people might muse: "Personality conflicts are a fact of life. You can't legislate them out of existence."

What happens if you scoff at the subjectivity of jerkiness and pass your Anti-Jerk Law anyway? All of the following:

1. Bosses try to avoid the *appearance* of jerkiness. But bosses with poor social skills or bad luck still get sued.

2. Since bosses try to avoid the appearance of jerkiness, litigious employees don't have a lot to work with.

3. As long as judges and juries are sympathetic, however, they lower the de facto burden of proof, allowing the war on jerks to continue indefinitely.

4. Bosses, in turn, defend themselves by trying to pre-emptively discredit litigious employees.

5. Cynical bosses go a step further by trying not to hire employees who are relatively likely to cry "jerk."

6. Human resource departments institute Orwellian anti-jerk training, where participants get punished for pointing out that the HR folks are domineering and insulting. In other words, HR reps exemplify the very thing they claim to oppose.

7. If so-called jerky managerial styles enhance productivity (think: athletic coaches), society forfeits major benefits.

As far as I know, no country has an Anti-Jerk Law in place. But many countries ban "discrimination," and the effects are much the same. Once you pass discrimination laws...

1. Bosses try to avoid the *appearance* of discrimination. But

bosses with poor social skills or bad luck still get sued.

2. Since bosses try to avoid the appearance of discrimination, litigious employees don't have a lot to work with.

3. As long as judges and juries are sympathetic, however, they lower the de facto burden of proof, allowing the war on discrimination to continue indefinitely.

4. Bosses, in turn, defend themselves by trying to pre-emptively discredit litigious employees.

5. Cynical bosses go a step further by trying not to hire employees who are relatively likely to cry "discrimination."

6. Human resource departments institute Orwellian anti-discrimination training, where participants get punished for pointing out that the HR folks are hostile and bigoted.[2] In other words, HR reps exemplify the very thing they claim to oppose.

7. If so-called discrimination enhances productivity (think: standardized testing), society forfeits major benefits.

Why do the same patterns emerge in both cases? Because "he discriminated against me" is about as subjective as "he was a jerk to me." In both cases, they *feel* very real to the accuser. In both cases, they *feel* very unfair to the accused. If you knew neither party, you'd probably decline to even express an opinion.

And with good reason.

November 23, 2020

* * *

14

Notes

1. Caplan, Bryan. "Being Normal." *EconLog*, November 10, 2020.
2. Caplan, Bryan. "The Uniformity and Exclusion Movement." *EconLog*, August 5, 2020.

The Punchline of Labor Market Regulation

L ast night, while rewatching the classic *Simpsons* "Saddlesore Galactica," I came across a great pedagogical moment that even *Homer Economicus: The Simpsons and Economics* misses.[1] In the episode, an abusive horse trainer flees from the state fair, leaving his mistreated equine behind. Hilarity ensues:

> **Officer Wiggum:** I'm afraid this horse is going to the dog food factory.
>
> **Homer:** Good luck getting a horse to eat dog food.
>
> **Bart:** You can't do that to Duncan. It's not his fault that his owner was a sleaze.
>
> **Officer Wiggum:** Look. I just want the horse to have a good home or be food. If you want to take him, fine with me.

Though the *Simpsons* writers almost surely didn't intend this as a critique of labor market regulation, the shoe fits. Imagine

Officer Wiggum on...

The minimum wage: "Look. I just want the worker to make $15 an hour or be unemployed."

Health insurance mandates: "Look. I just want the worker to have free medical care or be unemployed."

Firing restrictions: "Look. I just want the worker to have complete job security or be unemployed."

Could legally imposing these stark ultimatums be good strategy for pro-worker policy-makers? Anything's possible. The point is that stark ultimatums are a double-edged sword, not a no-brainer. A devoted horse-lover really could sensibly favor an option in between "good home" and "food." A friend of the workers really could sensibly oppose the minimum wage. It all depends on something almost no human being even understands, much less measures: elasticities.[2]

November 3, 2015

* * *

Notes

1. Hall, Joshua, ed. *Homer Economicus: The Simpsons and Economics*. Stanford, California: Stanford University Press, 2014.
2. Caplan, Bryan. "Making Populism Serious: The Case of Social Security." *EconLog*, August 16, 2012.

The Grave Evil of Unemployment

F ree-market economists rarely declare, "We have to do X about unemployment." Why not? Free-market economists' standard reply is just, "We expect X to fail." Their critics, however, have a less favorable explanation: Free-market economists oppose X because free-market economists are cavalier and callous. They cavalierly deny the reality of involuntary unemployment, and callously belittle the suffering of the unemployed.

I know hundreds of free-market economists. They're friends of mine. Indeed, I'm a free-market economist myself. It saddens me to say, then, that our critics are often right. While some free-market economists merely doubt the efficacy of policies intended to alleviate unemployment, the *average* free-market economist doesn't take the unemployment problem seriously.

Why not? At the level of high theory, free-market economists love market-clearing models. If there's surplus wheat, the price of wheat will fall to clear the market. If there's surplus labor, similarly, the wage will fall to eliminate unemployment. What about nominal wage rigidity? Most free-market economists concede that nominal wage rigidity exists to some degree, but think the problem is mild and short-lived: "It's been three years. The labor market must have fully adjusted by now."

High theory aside, though, free-market economists have a toolbox of quips they use to belittle the problem of unemployment.

There's the argument from the safety net: "Why would anyone want to go back to work when he can collect 99 weeks of unemployment insurance?"

There's the argument from relocation: "There are plenty of jobs in North Dakota. Anyone who refuses to move there is therefore *voluntarily* unemployed."

There's the argument from worker hubris: "If he's an 'unemployed carpenter,' then I'm an 'unemployed astronaut.'"

There's the argument from Zero Marginal Product: "If the guy can't find a job, his labor must be worthless."[1]

I'd be delighted if my fellow free-market economists' high theory and belittling quips were entirely correct. But they aren't. The high theory's wrong: Nominal wage rigidity is both strong and durable.[2] And the quips are far less insightful than they sound. Yes, unemployment insurance discourages job search; but this hardly means that most unemployed people affirmatively prefer the dole to a job. Yes, the unemployed could move to North Dakota; but in a market-clearing model of the labor market, workers wouldn't have to flee their state to sell their skills. Yes, some workers overestimate their own abilities; but the typical unemployed carpenter is competent in his craft. Yes, many workers have low marginal products; but almost no one has a marginal product of *zero*.[3]

Once you admit the severity and durability of nominal rigidities, it's hard to avoid the conclusion that much unemployment is involuntary. And once you admit that much unemployment is involuntary, it's hard to avoid the conclusion that unemployment is a serious problem. In terms of standard cost-benefit analysis, nominal rigidities have the same effects as price floors. Society loses the difference between each involuntarily unemployed worker's marginal product and his reservation wage.

Yet on further reflection, simple cost-benefit analysis grossly understates the horrors of unemployment. We should also consider the effect of unemployment on *happiness*. When workers don't get a raise, they're often disappointed or angry. But when workers lose their jobs, they literally *weep*. For most of us, a job isn't only a paycheck. A job also provides a sense of identity, purpose, and community. Happiness research strongly supports this fact, but introspection should suffice.[4] Think about the shame and despair you'd feel if you were suddenly unable to support your children.

Free-market economists should be especially dismayed by the cultural and political effects of unemployment. When every able-bodied worker can easily find a place to sell his skills, the economy reveals a clear connection between moral desert and practical success. You can fairly dismiss many complaints about capitalism by harumphing, "Get a job!" Workers can proudly tell statist activists and intellectuals, "I don't need your charity. I can take care of myself just fine." Once people lose their confidence that every able-bodied person can easily take care of himself, this individualist ethos withers – and the welfare state grows like a weed.

Instead of downplaying the grave evil of unemployment, we free-market economists should urge governments to redouble their efforts to fight it. How can we do so and remain free-market economists? First and foremost, by emphasizing the obvious: Every government imposes a vast array of employment-destroying regulations. Minimum wages.[5] Licensing laws. Pro-union laws. Mandated benefits – especially mandated health insurance.[6] Anyone who appreciates the grave evil of unemployment should bitterly oppose these regulations – and vigorously reject the cavalier, callous view that a heavy-duty safety net is a good substitute for a job.[7] Government regulation is hardly the sole cause of nominal wage rigidity, but it definitely makes a bad situation worse.

At this point, good Keynesians will object, "Asking government to stop exacerbating nominal wage rigidity is a fine start. But what about old-fashioned Aggregate Demand policies?"[8] There's no reason for free-market economists to fear this question. Tax cuts – especially tax cuts on employers – increase Aggregate Demand and employment, and they're as free-market as Frederic Bastiat.[9]

Isn't monetary policy a far more effective and sustainable way to boost Aggregate Demand?[10] Sure. Given the existence of a central bank, though, it's hard to see why free-market economists should run away from this conclusion. How is Nominal GDP targeting any less free-market than constant growth in M2, or a frozen monetary base, or short-run interest-rate targeting? If, as seems highly likely, Scott Sumner is right to blame the Great Recession on central banks' tight monetary policies, free-market economists should not be afraid to honor him.[11] Imagine how much statist legislation could have been averted if the world's central banks had kept NGDP on a steady course from 2008 to the present.

I'm proud to call myself a free-market economist. But free-market economics can and should improve. Our cavalier and callous attitudes about unemployment are deeply misguided.

Free-market economists should eagerly share their insights on how to alleviate the grave evil of unemployment instead of putting their heads in the sand and calling idle misery "optimal."

April 23, 2013

* * *

Notes

1. Caplan, Bryan. "ZMP, Morale, and Statistical Discrimination." *EconLog*, April 18, 2013.
2. Caplan, Bryan. "Long-Run Unemployment at Low Inflation: Dourado vs. Akerlof-Dickens-Perry." *EconLog*, September 19, 2012.
3. Caplan, Bryan. "The Reasons for My Hostility to ZMP." *EconLog*, November 17, 2011.
4. Caplan, Bryan. "The Joy of Market-Clearing Wages." *EconLog*, April 1, 2005.
5. Caplan, Bryan. "The Myopic Empiricism of the Minimum Wage." *EconLog*, March 12, 2013.
6. Caplan, Bryan. "The Long Run Is Nigh: Drum, Krugman, Disemployment and Obamacare." *EconLog*, January 5, 2012.
7. Caplan, Bryan. "Unemployment, Labor Market Regulation, and Sour Grapes." *EconLog*, May 26, 2009.
8. Caplan, Bryan. "'Wages Must Fall!': What All Good Keynesians Should Say." *EconLog*, December 15, 2011.
9. Caplan, Bryan. "Payroll Tax Hikes, Keynesianism, and the Recession: A Reply to Drum and Krugman." *EconLog*,

July 17, 2009.

10. Caplan, Bryan. "The Size of Monetary Stimulus vs. the Length of Monetary Stimulus." *EconLog*, August 30, 2011.

11. *TheMoneyIllusion*. "FAQs," n.d.

The Happy Hypocrisy of Unpaid Internships

L et me begin, like virtually every writer on unpaid internships, by blockquoting the Department of Labor's rules about such positions' permissibility.[1] Unpaid internships in the for-profit sector are allowed as long as *all* of the following are true:

1. The internship, even though it includes actual operation of the facilities of the employer, is similar to training which would be given in an educational environment;

2. The internship experience is for the benefit of the intern;

3. The intern does not displace regular employees, but works under close supervision of existing staff;

4. The employer that provides the training derives no immediate advantage from the activities of the intern; and on occasion its operations may actually be impeded;

5. The intern is not necessarily entitled to a job at the conclusion of the internship; and

6. The employer and the intern understand that

> the intern is not entitled to wages for the time spent
> in the internship.

Unlike virtually every writer on unpaid internships, I'm not going to suggest that many unpaid internships in the for-profit sector are illegal because they run afoul of one or more of these rules. Instead, I'm going to categorically state: *No unpaid internship in the for-profit sector ever has or ever will satisfy these rules!* Why? Because Rule #4 is absurd beyond belief.

Simple question: Why on earth would a *for-profit* firm hire interns from whom the firm derives "no immediate advantage"? Imagine you're a human resources officer at a firm and you want to launch an unpaid internship program. How would the Board of Directors respond if you declared, "I propose hiring unpaid interns from whom we derive no immediate advantage whatsoever"? What would they think if you added, "Oh, and these interns will occasionally impede our operations"? The Board's obvious reaction would be, "We're a business, not a charity." No profit-maximizing firm would want to hire unpaid interns under the written rules.

The absurdity of Rule #3 isn't quite as blatant, but no firm complies with it either. Anything useful an intern does *could* have been done by a regular employee. Don't believe me? Fire the interns and see who picks up the slack. Of course, if it's compliant with Rule #4, no intern can do anything useful for the firm anyway.

Mainstream writers on unpaid internships take it for granted that rule-breaking internships must be stopped. Many would be delighted to use my observations to ban unpaid internships altogether. My point, of course, is the opposite: Rules this stupid are made to be broken.[2] Hypocrisy and double-talk shield us from the malevolent folly of the Department of Labor.

What makes these rules so stupid? Simple: Internships are vocational education. If schools can educate students in exchange for their tuition, why can't businesses educate students in exchange for their labor? No reason, just anti-market bigotry.

The real problem with unpaid internships is that we're not hypocritical enough. Regulators look the other way when businesses train college students for college-type jobs in exchange for their labor. But the rest of the labor market is out of luck. If McDonald's set up unpaid internships for high school dropouts, regulators would come down on it like a ton of bricks. As a result, the only people who can get on-the-job training are those who need it the least. Instead of banning unpaid internships, we should make them available to everyone.

P.S. Does this mean we should abolish the minimum wage?[3] Well, if there's a good reason why trainees should get either $0.00 or $7.25 but nothing in between, I'd like to hear it.

P.P.S.: Nathaniel Bechhofer points out that John Stossel made a related point some years ago.[4]

August 24, 2015

* * *

Notes

1. "Fact Sheet #71: Internship Programs Under The Fair Labor Standards Act." U.S. Department of Labor Wage and Hour Division, January 2018.
2. Caplan, Bryan. "The Righteous Scofflaw." *EconLog*, April 8, 2014.
3. Caplan, Bryan. "The Myopic Empiricism of the Minimum Wage." *EconLog*, March 12, 2013.
4. Stossel, John. "Unpaid Interns Are Exploited?" *Reason.com*, May 6, 2010.

Labor Demand Elasticity: Boredom is Thoughtless

When workers are cheaper, employers want more. But how *many* more? Does a 1% fall in the price of labor entice .1% higher employment? .5% more? 1% more? In technical terms, what is labor's elasticity of demand? So much hinges on this seemingly boring question – everything from "How pro-worker is 'pro-worker' legislation?" to "Does the minimum wage, on balance, help low-skilled workers?" to "Are wage cuts a credible solution to mass unemployment?" to "What is the effect of immigration on native wages?"[1]

The empirical literature, as you'd expect, is vast. But in 2015, the *European Economic Review* published a major meta-analysis.[2] This edifying piece begins with the distribution of earlier findings:

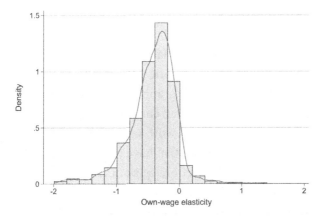

Notice: As expected, labor demand elasticity has a negative slope, with modal estimates around -.4. But Lichter et al. naturally aren't satisfied with a histogram. They break the results down by time period (short-run, intermediate-run, and long-run elasticity), model, dataset, and workforce characteristics.

Highlights of their big page of results (using absolute value for convenience, so "higher elasticity"= "a more negative elasticity"):

- Long-run elasticity is noticeably higher than short-run elasticity, a gap of .3 in the simple model and .15 in the full model.
- Panel data yields elasticities about .25 higher than other data.
- Demand for low-skilled, female, and atypical employment is markedly more elastic, an extra .21, .17. and .54 respectively.

Additional result: Labor demand is more elastic in countries with less labor regulation!

Fig. 4 plots the predicted labor demand elasticities against the country-specific OECD Employment Legislation Index. The graph shows a positive relationship between overall employment protection and the wage elasticity, with labor demand being less elastic in countries that have rather strict rules of employment protection legislation (for example, Spain and Mexico). In contrast, labor demand is more elastic in those countries that have weak rules on employment protection (for example, the UK and Canada). Differences in employment protection legislation among countries may thus contribute to the country-specific estimates of the labor demand elasticity.

The graph:

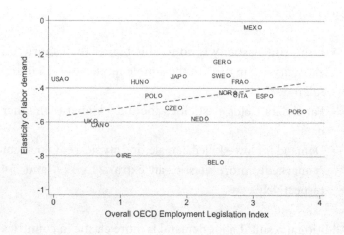

The authors conclude by testing for publication bias and find fairly convincing evidence that researchers are hunting for statistical significance. The published paper leaves it at that, but the working paper includes "publication bias corrected" estimates:

> Our preferred estimate in terms of specification - the long-run, constant output elasticity obtained from a structural-form model using administrative panel data at the rm level for the latest mean year of observation, with mean characteristics on all other variables and corrected for publication selection bias - is -0.246, bracketed by the interval [-0.072;-0.446]. Compared to this interval, we note that (i) many estimates of the own-wage elasticity of labor demand given in the literature are upwardly inflated (with a mean value larger than -0.5 in absolute terms) and (ii) our preferred estimate is close to the best guess provided by Hamermesh (1993), albeit with our confidence interval for values of the elasticity being smaller.[3]

Who cares? In practice, almost no one. Twitter mentions for "labor demand elasticity" average about one per *month*! No politician who yearns for victory addresses this "boring" topic. But if people actually cared about the effects of labor market regulation on worker and human well-being, labor demand elasticity would fascinate them. An elasticity of -.25 implies that raising wages 4% permanently depresses employment by 1%. Considering the misery of involuntary unemployment and our hedonic adaptation to mere money, how can any thoughtful person yawn?[4]

August 17, 2016

* * *

Notes

1. Caplan, Bryan. "Labor Econ Versus the World: Ecumenical Edition." *EconLog*, December 23, 2015.; Caplan, Bryan. "The Myopic Empiricism of the Minimum Wage." *EconLog*, March 12, 2013.; Caplan, Bryan. "The Grave Evil of Unemployment." *EconLog*, April 23, 2013.; Caplan, Bryan. "An Infinite Contradiction." *EconLog*, May 19, 2005.

2. Lichter, Andreas, Andreas Peichl, and Sebastian Siegloch. "The Own-Wage Elasticity of Labor Demand: A Meta-Regression Analysis." *European Economic Review* 80 (November 2015): 94–119.

3. Lichter, Andreas, Andreas Peichl, and Sebastian Siegloch. "The Own-Wage Elasticity of Labor Demand: A Meta-Regression Analysis," 19. IZA Institute of Labor Economics, 2014.

4. Caplan, Bryan. "The Joy of Market-Clearing Wages." *EconLog*, April 1, 2005.

Mentoring: The Rationality of Fear

Some months ago, Lean In published the results of a survey by Sandberg and Pritchard showing a dramatic increase in the share of male managers who fear close interaction with female coworkers. Specifically:

> 60% of managers who are men are uncomfortable participating in a common work activity with a woman, such as mentoring, working alone, or socializing together. That's a 32% jump from a year ago.[1]

The survey's creators were dismayed:

> This is disastrous. The vast majority of managers and senior leaders are men. They have a huge role to play in supporting women's advancement at work—or hindering it… There's not a company in the world that can afford to leave talent on the sidelines because that talent is female. But that's what will keep happening unless all of us—especially men—commit to doing better.[2]

Most commentators found male managers' reluctance to mentor women especially reprehensible and irrational.[3] Male managers aren't just undermining gender equality; they're paranoid. How so? Because innocent men have nothing to fear except false accusations – and these hardly ever happen. Thus, Prudy Gourguechon remarks:

> The implication of the surveys is that men are afraid of being falsely accused. But false accusations of sexual impropriety are actually very rare.[4]

Mia Brett tells us:

> Despite the framing of this story, male managers refusing to mentor women started long before #MeToo. Furthermore, fears of false accusation aren't supported by statistics.[5]

Andrew Fiouzi:

> [D]ealing with men's unrealistic fears around false accusations will require unfamiliar amounts of self-reflection on the part of the men in question.[6]

Emily Peck:

> Some men also like to claim that women are fabricating claims. Those fears are largely unfounded, Thomas said. She points out that the same myth surrounds sexual assault. False accusations make up a very low percentage of reported rapes, according

to several studies — in line with other types of crime.[7]

While it's dauntingly hard to credibly estimate the rate of false accusation, I suspect all the preceding authors are correct. Human beings rarely invent bald harmful lies about others.

On reflection, however, this hardly implies that male managers are paranoid or otherwise "irrational." For three reasons:

1. You have to multiply the probability of a false accusation by the *harm* of a false accusation. Since the harm is high, even a seemingly negligible probability may be worth worrying about. Consider this passage in Fiouzi's analysis:

> But according to Richard J. Reddick, an associate professor of educational leadership and policy at the University of Texas at Austin, there is, practically speaking, no evidence to justify the Pence Rule [not dining alone with women other than your wife]. "You often hear about men being falsely accused of sexual harassment," he says. "[But] the University of California, San Diego Center on Gender Equity and Health conducted a study recently that revealed that two percent of men and one percent of women had been falsely accused of sexual harassment or assault, so in fact, accusations, and particularly false ones, are exceptionally rare."

Taking these estimates at face value, it's hard to see the paranoia: A 2% chance of severe career damage is a *serious* risk, especially given the low personal benefits of mentoring.

Furthermore, managers are far more tempting targets for false accusation than ordinary co-workers, so their probability of being falsely accused plausibly rises to 4%, 6%, or even 10%.

2. In any case, a low *rate* of false accusation multiplied by a *long* mentoring career could still readily lead to *multiple* false accusations. So it's hardly imprudent for many male managers to respond with great caution. Remember: The chance you'll die in a car crash today if you don't wear a seat belt is a rounding error. The chance you'll eventually die in a car crash if you *habitually* don't wear a seat belt, however, is nothing to scoff at.

3. As I've explained before, truly malevolent actions – such as falsely accusing others – are far less common than *misunderstandings*.[8] Misunderstandings are a ubiquitous un-pleasant feature of human life. One common way to avoid this unpleasantness is to avoid social situations likely to lead to misunderstandings. This strategy is especially tempting if, in the event of a misunderstanding, others will presume you're in the wrong. So again, it's hardly surprising that many male managers would respond to changing norms (#BelieveWomen) by playing defense.

What then should be done? The emotionally appealing response, sadly, is to fight fear with an extra helping of fear: "You're too scared to mentor? Interesting. Now let me show you what we do to those who shirk their mentoring responsibilities." If this seems like a caricature, carefully listen to what the authors of the original survey have to say:

> Ugly behavior that once was indulged or ignored is
> finally being called out and condemned. Now we

must go further. Avoiding and isolating women at work—whether out of an overabundance of caution, a misguided sense of decorum, irritation at having to check your words or actions, or any other reason—must be unacceptable too.

The problem, of course, is that mentoring is too informal to easily monitor. Unless someone loudly announces, "I refuse to mentor women," there's not much you can do to him. Mentoring quotas are likely to flop for the same reason.

The alternative is obvious, but unpalatable for activists: *Put the frightened people whose assistance you need at ease.* Be friendly and calm, gracious and grateful. Take the ubiquity of misunderstandings seriously. Don't zealously advocate for yourself, and don't rush to take sides. Instead, strive to deescalate conflict whenever a misunderstanding arises. This would obviously work best as a coordinated cultural shift toward good manners, but you don't have to wait for the world to come to its senses.[9] You can start building your personal reputation for collegiality today – so why wait to get potential mentors on your side?

If you're tempted to respond, "Why should *I* have to put *them* at ease?," the honest answer is: Because you're the one asking for help.

If that's the way you talk to others, though, don't expect them to give you honest answers. Intimidation is the father of silence and the mother of lies. If you have to use threats to exhort help, you'll probably just get a bunch of empty promises.

February 5, 2020

* * *

Notes

1. Lean In. "Key Findings: Working Relationships in the #MeToo Era," n.d.
2. Sandberg, Sheryl, and Marc Pritchard. "The Number of Men Who Are Uncomfortable Mentoring Women Is Growing." *Fortune*, May 17, 2019.
3. McGregor, Jena. "#MeToo Backlash: More Male Managers Avoid Mentoring Women or Meeting Alone with Them." *The Washington Post*, May 17, 2019.
4. Gourguechon, Prudy. "Why In The World Would Men Stop Mentoring Women Post #MeToo?" *Forbes*, August 6, 2018.
5. Brett, Mia. "Many in Media Distort the Framing of #MeToo." *Women's Media Center*, July 24, 2019.
6. Fiouzi, Andrew. "Here's What We Can Do About Men Who Don't Want to Mentor Women in the Era of #MeToo." *MEL Magazine*, August 23, 2019.
7. Peck, Emily. "Me Too Backlash Is Getting Worse." *HuffPost*, May 17, 2019.
8. Caplan, Bryan. "Malevolence and Misunderstanding." *EconLog*, September 17, 2019.
9. Caplan, Bryan. "Good Manners vs. Political Correctness." *EconLog*, March 23, 2017.

Funny Bargains

The worker-employer bargain has many funny features.[1] Scott Alexander points out a few:

1. Employers sometimes yell at workers for small mistakes; workers aren't supposed to yell at employers no matter how big the employers' mistakes.

2. Employers sometimes demand job applicants' bodily fluids; applicants fear to ask prospective employers for a cup of coffee.

3. Employers sometimes demand that workers stay late; workers rarely demand to leave early.[2]

Scott takes these as strong symptoms that the supply-and-demand model of labor markets is deeply wrong. The asymmetries exist because each worker needs his employer a lot more than his employer needs him.

Now let's consider two other bargains with similarly funny features. First, the patron-waiter relationship.

1. Patrons sometimes yell at waiters for small mistakes; waiters aren't supposed to yell at customers no matter what.

2. Patrons sometimes ask waiters for elaborate special

treatment (e.g. no nuts, extra nuts, sauce on the side, gluten-free sauce...); waiters aren't supposed to ask patrons for the smallest favor (e.g. a tiny bite of their dessert, or "Kindly eat over your plate").

3. No matter how diligent waiters are, customers are still allowed to tip them zero.

Second, consider the customer-Big Box Store relationship.

1. Customers can buy an item, try it, decide they don't like it, then get a full refund.

2. Customers can ask store employees to help them find a product, but store employees would never ask customers to help them stock the shelves – even for a minute.

3. Customers can be rude to the store manager, but the store manager still has to be polite to customers.

In all three cases, of course, economists have a standard mantra: *it's all reflected in the price.* If being an employer is pleasant and being a worker is unpleasant, labor demand goes up, labor supply goes down, and the wage goes up. If being a patron is pleasant and being a waiter is unpleasant, demand goes up, supply goes down, and the price of restaurant meals goes up. If store customers and stores know they can return anything they don't like, demand goes up, supply goes down, and the price of store products goes up. Why exactly is it so important to restaurant patrons that waiters never ask them for a bite of their dessert? Norms, psychology, and status all play a role. But as long as asymmetric conditions are reflected in the price, who cares about their source?

September 4, 2015

* * *

Notes

1. Caplan, Bryan. "Scott Alexander on Labor Economics: Point-by-Point Reply." *EconLog*, September 2, 2015.
2. Alexander, Scott. "The Non-Libertarian FAQ." *Slate Star Codex*, February 23, 2017.; Caplan, Bryan. "Scott Alexander on Labor Economics." *EconLog*, September 1, 2015.

"Wages Must Fall!": What All Good Keynesians Should Say

When Keynesians want to gloat, they often point to the overwhelming empirical evidence in favor of nominal wage rigidity. For the latest example, see Krugman on the Irish labor market.[1] Their unemployment is 14.5%, but the nominal wage index has only fallen by about 2.5%. Krugman's conclusion:

> It is really, really hard to cut nominal wages, which is why reliance on "internal devaluation" is a recipe for stagnation and disaster.

The gloating is easy to understand. After all, nominal wage rigidity is the driving assumption of the Keynesian model.[2] Unemployment is just a labor surplus; since wages are the price of labor, the fundamental cause of unemployment has to be excessive wages. And as long as the wage rigidity is nominal, you can neutralize it by printing money or otherwise boosting demand.

What's hard to understand, though, is Keynesian neglect of – if not outright hostility to – the logical implication of their argument: Wages must fall! If they're right about nominal wage rigidity, it seems like "Wages must fall!" would be the mantra of all good Keynesians. But few words are less likely to escape their lips.

Why would this be so?

1. Keynesians could say that nominal wage rigidity is such an intractable problem there's no point discussing it. That's why Krugman emphasizes that "Ireland is supposed to have flexible markets — remember, before the crisis it was hailed as an example of successful structural reform." If wages won't even fall in laissez-faire Ireland, what hope does the rest of the world have?

There are two big problems with this story.

(a) Even if it's true, Keynesians should still militantly oppose any government policy – like the employer health care mandate – that increases labor costs.

(b) Government doesn't face a binary choice between conventional labor market regulation and laissez-faire. There's a third choice: Low-wage interventionism. If wages won't adjust on their own, why don't Keynesians ask government to actively *push them down*? If that sounds too brutal, see Singapore for clever ways to numb the blow.[3]

2. Keynesians could say that monetary and fiscal policy are easier to promote than wage cuts. But Keynesians are the first to insist that fiscal policy is a valuable supplement to monetary policy. Why not hail wage cuts as a valuable supplement to both? At minimum, Keynesians should heatedly resist any government policy that pushes labor costs in the wrong

direction – and remind us that "wrong" = up.

3. Keynesians could – and often do – retreat to the view that wage flexibility is a self-defeating solution to the problem of wage rigidity.[4] The idea is that wage cuts reduce demand, which in turn exacerbates unemployment.

But this argument is full of holes. As I've pointed out before, there are strong reasons to think that wage cuts will *increase* aggregate demand, making this solution doubly attractive.[5] Consider: Labor income equals wages multiplied by hours worked, so the effect on labor income is ambiguous; and as a matter of pure arithmetic, lower wages imply higher profit income. In any case, if nominal wage cuts really are as rare as a blue moon, what makes Keynesians so sure that wage cuts would backfire if tried? Without lots of empirical counter-examples, they have every reason to stick to the common sense position: "If wage rigidity is the cause of unemployment, wage flexibility is the cure."

At this point, Keynesians could just bite the bullet: "Wages must fall!" But in my experience they don't – and I don't think they're going to start now. The reason, I'm afraid, is politics. Keynesians lean left. They don't want to say, "Wages must fall!" They don't want to think it. "Wages must fall!" sounds reactionary – a thinly-veiled reproach to centuries of anti-capitalist intellectuals and militant unions. After all, doesn't it mean that every "pro-labor" regulation and "victory for the workers" has an ugly downside – more workers unable to find any job at all?[6]

Keynesians are right to ridicule people who deny the reality of nominal wage rigidity.[7] But they'd be a lot more persuasive if they put leftist qualms aside and focused on the logic of their own model. Keynesians have every reason to rant against excessive wages. They have every reason to rant against regulation that increases labor costs. They have every reason to rant against unions. And there hasn't been a better time to rant since the Great Depression. Oh my Keynesian brothers and sisters, let us rant together.

December 31, 2011

* * *

Notes

1. Krugman, Paul. "Lessons From Europe." *The New York Times*, December 10, 2012.
2. Caplan, Bryan. "Labor Market Rigidity: Psychology, Technology, and Peter Pan." *EconLog*, May 15, 2010.
3. Caplan, Bryan. "Singapore: 'Automatic Stabilizers' Done Right." *EconLog*, January 11, 2008.
4. Krugman, Paul. "Falling Wage Syndrome." *The New York Times*, May 3, 2009.
5. Caplan, Bryan. "Why Wage Cuts Are Good For Aggregate Demand." *EconLog*, May 7, 2009.
6. Caplan, Bryan. "The Joy of Market-Clearing Wages." *EconLog*, April 1, 2005.
7. Akerlof, George, William Dickens, and George Perry. "The Macroeconomics of Low Inflation." *Brookings Papers on Economic Activity* (1996): 1–59.

Why Wage Cuts Are Good For Aggregate Demand

K rugman's repeating his argument that wage cuts are individually rational, but collectively irrational:

> [M]any workers are accepting pay cuts in order to save jobs. What's wrong with that? The answer lies in one of those paradoxes that plague our economy right now. We're suffering from the paradox of thrift: saving is a virtue, but when everyone tries to sharply increase saving at the same time, the effect is a depressed economy... And soon we may be facing the paradox of wages: workers at any one company can help save their jobs by accepting lower wages, but when employers across the economy cut wages at the same time, the result is higher unemployment.[1]

If you're really anti-Krugman, you might think he's saying that, "Wage cuts reduce labor income, which reduces aggregate demand." If this is his argument, it has two major problems:

1. Cutting wages increases the quantity of labor demanded. If

labor demand is elastic, total labor income *rises* as a result of wage cuts.

2. Even if labor demand is inelastic, moreover, wage cuts reduce labor income by raising *employers'* income. So unless employers are unusually likely to put cash under their mattresses, wage cuts *still* boost aggregate demand.

But is Krugman even making an argument about aggregate demand? At first glance, it doesn't look like it:

> Here's how the paradox works. Suppose that work-ers at the XYZ Corporation accept a pay cut. That lets XYZ management cut prices, making its prod-ucts more competitive. Sales rise, and more workers can keep their jobs. So you might think that wage cuts raise employment — which they do at the level of the individual employer. But if everyone takes a pay cut, nobody gains a competitive advantage. So there's no benefit to the economy from lower wages.

Alas, this still leaves me saying, *"No benefit*?! Huh?"* Won't consumers benefit when there's more cheap stuff? In purely Keynesian terms, too, there's a real balance effect. The most that Krugman could reasonably say is that wage cuts have underappreciated drawbacks. What are these supposed to be?

1. "[F]alling wages, and hence falling incomes, worsen the problem of excessive debt." *Now* Krugman really does seem to blithely assume that reducing wages reduces aggregate demand. And I have to respond: "Do falling wages worsen the problem more than higher unemployment due to wage

rigidity?"

2. Krugman also warns that falling wages might lead consumers to expect further wage declines, effectively raising real interest rates – "And a rise in the effective interest rate is the last thing this economy needs." I grant that this *might* happen if wage cuts continued for a long time, and could conceivably be bad if it happened. But for now, this is paranoia.

It's also worth pointing out that in a standard New Keynesian textbook model, higher inflationary expectations reduce aggregate supply and worsen the inflation-unemployment trade-off. Corollary: The straightforward effect of *lower* inflationary expectations is to increase aggregate supply and improve the inflation-unemployment trade-off.

I'm far from a knee-jerk Krugman basher.[2] I gleefully assign *The Accidental Theorist* to my undergraduate labor students.[3] But when Krugman forgets that wage rigidity is the fundamental cause of involuntary unemployment, a sound bashing is in order.

May 7, 2009

* * *

Notes

1. Krugman, Paul. "Falling Wage Syndrome." *The New York Times*, May 3, 2009.
2. Caplan, Bryan. "Paul Krugman, Guilty Pleasure." *Marginal Revolution* (blog), July 30, 2004.
3. Krugman, Paul. *The Accidental Theorist: And Other*

Dispatches from the Dismal Science. New York, NY: Norton, 1999.

Dehiring: Win-Win-Lose

Suppose your firm has a mediocre employee. He's not ridiculous, but he's worth a lot less than you pay him. What does your firm do?

Econ professors' knee-jerk answer is, "Fire him." But people with real jobs often notice a rather different reaction: Instead of firing the mediocre employee, his boss tells him, "You need to find other opportunities." The worker then has 1-3 months to search for another job, free of the stigma of current unemployment. In HR jargon, the firm "dehires" him. This how-to guide explains:

> Managing a problematic employee is time consuming and negatively affects the cohesion of your fitness team. Unfortunately, hoping that a troublesome employee will just go away is not always realistic and may even make the situation worse. Instead of backing away from the problem, take action. By learning how to "de-hire," you may never have to fire anyone again. [...] Begin the conversation with statements such as "Sue, it appears that Club X is really not the place you want to be working. You have been calling in sick and arguing with members.

Perhaps you're not happy teaching here any more?"
"Sue, are you truly happy at Club X or do you feel
you might need a change?" or "Sue, it doesn't appear
that you want to be part of the team anymore. Why
don't you think about what you want to do and let's
meet again tomorrow."[1]

Dehiring has two main advantages over firing. First, it is
legally safer. Employees who leave of their own volition to take
another position are far less likely to sue you than employees
you kick to the curb. Second, it is psychologically easier.[2]
When a firm fires a worker, his boss and co-workers feel
sorry for him. When a firm dehires a worker, his boss and
co-workers feel happy for themselves! No wonder the subtitle
of the how-to guide is: "Don't fire. Learn to de-hire to create
a win-win situation for you and your employee."

On reflection, though, dehiring is only "win-win" for the
firm and the worker. What about the problem worker's *next*
firm? Dehiring is a nefarious plot between the worker and
his current firm: "If you help me find another job, I'll become
their problem instead of yours." From the standpoint of the
next employer, calling dehiring "win-win" is a sick joke. The
proper description is "win-win-lose" – the worker wins, the
old firm wins, the new firm loses.

The prevalence of dehiring is another reason why educational signaling matters despite employer learning.[3] Suppose
workers become transparent to their employers after a year
on the job. If firms summarily fire subpar performers,
educational signals wouldn't matter long. But if firms with
subpar workers drag their feet, then dehire, educational signals
can matter indefinitely. The mediocre worker moves from

51

firm to firm, gradually exhausting the pity of his employer and co-workers. As long as he looks good on paper, everyone who knows the mediocre worker's true colors can escape by passing the buck to another unwitting employer.

Is there anything the government could do to ameliorate this problem?

Sure. The government could *mandate* disclosure: If another employer inquires about your current or former employee, you must reveal everything negative that you know about him. If you lie – or simply hold back – an employer who detrimentally relies on your reference can sue you for fraud.

As is often the case, though, actual government policy deliberately amplifies market inefficiency rather than mitigating it. Existing law doesn't punish firms for concealing negative information; it punishes firms for *revealing* negative information. The results are sadly predictable: Employers fear to hire – and when they do hire, verifiable credentials matter more than the dubious words of the people who already know the truth.

August 20, 2013

* * *

Notes

1. Popowych, Krista. "De-Hiring a Problem Employee." IDEA Health & Fitness Association, December 31, 2003.
2. Caplan, Bryan. "Firing Aversion: A Cross-Cultural Study." *EconLog*, June 4, 2012.

3. Caplan, Bryan. "The Magic of Education." *EconLog*, November 28, 2011.

The Myopic Empiricism of the Minimum Wage

U nlike most opponents of the minimum wage, I admit that David Card and Alan Krueger's famous research on the topic is well-done.[1] How then can I continue to embrace (and teach!) the textbook view that the minimum wage significantly reduces employment of low-skilled workers?

Part of the reason is admittedly my strong prior. In the absence of *any* specific empirical evidence, I am 99%+ sure that a randomly selected demand curve will have a negative slope. I hew to this prior even in cases – like demand for illegal drugs or illegal immigration – where a downward-sloping demand curve is ideologically inconvenient for me. What makes me so sure? Every purchase I've ever made or considered – and every conversation I've had with other people about every purchase they've ever made or considered.

Another reason why Card-Krueger hasn't flipped my position: Despite my admiration for their craftsmanship, even the best empirical social science isn't that good. I expect true theories to predict the data only two-thirds of the time – and false theories to predict the data one-third of the time. (N.B. Many of the weaknesses in empirical social science are systematic, so the Law of Large Numbers is no salvation). Bayesian upshot: The Card-Krueger findings only slightly reduce my initial high confidence that the minimum wage causes unemployment.

But suppose you disagree with me on both counts. Suppose you have a weak prior about the disemployment effects of the minimum wage. Suppose further that you think that the best empirical work in economics is very good indeed. Doesn't existing evidence then oblige you to admit that the minimum wage has roughly zero effect on employment?

Hardly. Why not? Because there is far more "existing evidence" than meets the eye. Research doesn't have to officially be about the minimum wage to be highly relevant to the debate. All of the following empirical literatures support the orthodox view that the minimum wage has pronounced disemployment effects:

1. *The literature on the effect of low-skilled immigration on native wages.* A strong consensus finds that large increases in low-skilled immigration have little effect on low-skilled native wages.[2] David Card himself is a major contributor here, most famously for his study of the Mariel boatlift.[3] These results imply a *highly elastic* demand curve for low-skilled labor, which in turn implies a large disemployment effect of the minimum wage.

This consensus among immigration researchers is so strong that George Borjas titled his dissenting paper "The Labor Demand Curve *Is* Downward Sloping."[4] If this were a paper on the minimum wage, readers would assume Borjas was arguing that the labor demand curve is downward-sloping rather than *vertical*. Since he's writing about immigration, however, he's actually claiming the labor demand curve is downward-sloping rather than *horizontal!*

2. *The literature on the effect of European labor market regulation.* Most economists who study European labor markets admit that strict labor market regulations are an important cause of high long-term unemployment.[5] When I ask random European economists, they tell me, "The economics is clear; the problem is politics," meaning that European governments are afraid to embrace the deregulation they know they need to restore full employment. To be fair, high minimum wages are only one facet of European labor market regulation. But if you find that one kind of regulation that raises labor costs reduces employment, the reasonable inference to draw is that *any* regulation that raises labor costs has similar effects – including, of course, the minimum wage.

3. *The literature on the effects of price controls in general.* There are vast empirical literatures studying the effects of price controls of housing (rent control), agriculture (price supports), energy (oil and gas price controls), banking (Regulation Q), etc. Each of these literatures bolsters the textbook story about the effect of price controls – and therefore ipso facto bolsters the textbook story about the effect of price controls in the labor market.

If you object, "Evidence on rent control is only relevant for housing markets, not labor markets," I'll retort, "In that case, evidence on the minimum wage in New Jersey and Pennsylvania in the 1990s is only relevant for those two states during that decade." My point: If you can't generalize empirical results from one market to another, you can't generalize empirical results from one state to another, or one era to another. And if that's what you think, empirical work is a waste of time.

4. *The literature on Keynesian macroeconomics.* If you're even mildly Keynesian, you know that downward nominal wage rigidity occasionally leads to lots of involuntary unemployment.[6] If, like most Keynesians, you think that your view is backed by overwhelming empirical evidence, I have a challenge for you: Explain why market-driven downward nominal wage rigidity leads to unemployment *without* implying that a government-imposed minimum wage leads to unemployment.[7] The challenge is tough because the whole point of the minimum wage is to intensify what Keynesians correctly see as the fundamental cause of unemployment: The failure of nominal wages to fall until the market clears.[8]

The minimum wage is far from the most harmful regulation on the books. Why then do I make such a big deal about it? Because it is a symbol of larger evils.

From the standpoint of public policy, the minimum wage is a symbol of the view that "feel-good" policies are viable solutions to social ills: "Workers aren't paid enough? Pass a law so employers have to pay them more. Problem solved." From the standpoint of social science, the minimum wage is a symbol of the myopic view that you can become an expert on X by reading nothing but the leading research that explicitly addresses X: "Does the minimum wage reduce employment? Read the top papers on the minimum wage. Problem solved."

We need to get rid of the minimum wage. But that's only a first step. Our ultimate goal should be to get rid of the errors that the minimum wage has come to represent.

March 12, 2013

* * *

Notes

1. Card, David, and Alan Krueger. "Minimum Wages and Employment: A Case Study of the Fast Food Industry in New Jersey and Pennsylvania." *American Economic Review* 84, no. 4 (September 1994): 772-93.
2. Kerr, Sari Pekkala, and William Kerr. "Economic Impacts of Immigration: A Survey." NBER Working Paper #16736, January 2011.
3. Card, David. "The Impact of the Mariel Boatlift on the Miami Labor Market." *ILR Review* 43, no. 2 (January 1990): 245–57.
4. Borjas, George. "The Labor Demand Curve *Is* Downward Sloping: Reexamining the Impact of Immigration on the Labor Market." *Quarterly Journal of Economics* 118, no. 4 (November 2003): 1335-74.
5. Siebert, Horst. "Labor Market Rigidities: At the Root of Unemployment in Europe." *Journal of Economic Perspectives* 11, no. 3 (Summer 1997): 37–54.
6. Caplan, Bryan. "Long-Run Unemployment at Low Inflation: Dourado vs. Akerlof-Dickens-Perry." *EconLog*, September 19, 2012.
7. Caplan, Bryan. "The Keynesian Attraction." *EconLog*, October 1, 2010.
8. Caplan, Bryan. "'Wages Must Fall!': What All Good Keynesians Should Say." *EconLog*, December 15, 2011.

An Infinite Contradiction

avid Card has a new study arguing that immigration has basically no effect on the wages of domestic low-skilled workers.[1] This confirms his earlier results on the famed Mariel boatlift, when Castro freed 125,000 Cubans to flee to Miami.[2]

Is this result theoretically possible? How can the supply of labor increase, but leave wages unchanged? Card has little patience for these questions:

"As the evidence has accumulated over the past two decades that local labor market outcomes are only weakly correlated with immigrant densities, some analysts have argued that the cross-city research design is inherently compromised by intercity mobility of people, goods, and services. Underlying this argument is the belief that labor market competition posed by immigration has to affect native opportunities, so if we don't find an impact, the research design must be flawed."

A better answer, though, would have been to go to the blackboard. Card's results are theoretically possible. All that is necessary, as Figure 1 shows, is that labor demand be infinitely elastic, i.e., horizontal.

Figure 1: Infinitely Elastic Labor Demand

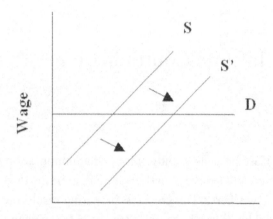

Quantity of Labor

Notice: When the Supply curve shifts out, the quantity of labor sold increases, and wages stay the same.

But this gets me thinking. Card is of course the co-author, with Alan Krueger, of the legendary study of the fast-food industry in Pennsylvania and New Jersey showing that the minimum wage does not reduce employment. Their book goes further, debunking earlier studies that found the opposite.[3]

Is *this* result theoretically possible? How can the minimum price of labor increase, but leave employment unchanged? Let's go back to the blackboard.

It turns out that Card and Krueger's results are theoretically possible too. All that is necessary, as Figure 2 shows, is that labor demand be infinitely inelastic, i.e., vertical. (The thick horizontal line between S and D at the controlled price is a labor surplus, but note that the quantity of labor purchased remains unchanged).

Figure 2: Infinitely Inelastic Labor Demand

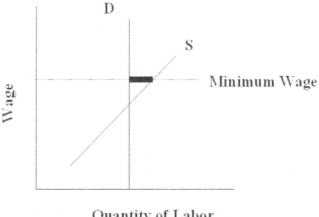

Quantity of Labor

David Card has a higher IQ than me. He taught my graduate micro class, and put me in my place, fair and square. But taken together, I have to conclude that *his research on immigration flatly contradicts his research on the minimum wage*. His results for immigration imply that labor demand is infinitely responsive to price; his results for the minimum wage imply that labor demand is not responsive to price at all.

You could say that my former teacher has two sets of results for two different kinds of markets. But in both cases, he's focused on markets for low-skill labor. Lots of immigrants from the Mariel boatlift presumably got jobs at McDonald's. He's not looking at two different markets; he's looking at roughly the same market from two different angles.

What gives? I think Card's work on immigration is closer

to the truth than his work on the minimum wage. But it's not because the immigration studies are well-done and the minimum wage studies are not. The quality of Card's empirical work is uniformly high. I simply find his results for immigration more intrinsically plausible.

Why? As a theoretical matter, demand is highly inelastic under two main conditions:

1. Total expenditure on the good is a small fraction of one's budget.

2. There are no good substitutes for the good.

In the market for low-skilled labor, neither assumption is credible. Labor expenses are usually the main cost of doing business. And you only have to peek over the counter at McDonald's to see how easily machines can replace men.

These simple observations are the main reason why I think immigration does not reduce domestic wages much, and the minimum wage has a substantial employment cost. It would take pretty strong empirical evidence to change my mind. A bunch of studies finding that labor demand is either infinitely elastic or infinitely inelastic don't come close.

May 19, 2005

* * *

Notes

1. Card, David. "Is the New Immigration Really So Bad?" *The Economic Journal* 115, no. 507 (November 2005): 300–323.
2. Card, David. "The Impact of the Mariel Boatlift on the

Miami Labor Market." *ILR Review* 43, no. 2 (January 1990): 245–57.

3. Card, David, and Alan Krueger. *Myth and Measurement: The New Economics of the Minimum Wage.* Princeton, NJ: Princeton Univ. Press, 1995.

The Minimum Wage vs. Welfare:
Band-Aid or Salt?

P eter Thiel entertains what economists would call a "second-best" argument in favor of raising the minimum wage:

> In theory, I'm against it, because people should have the freedom to contract at whatever wage they'd like to have. But in practice, I think the alternative to higher minimum wage is that people simply end up going on welfare. And so, given how low the minimum wage is — and how generous the welfare benefits are — you have a marginal tax rate that's on the order of 100 percent, and people are actually trapped in this sort of welfare state. So I actually think that it's a very out of the box idea — but it's something one should consider seriously, given all the other distorted incentives that exist.[1]

Is he right? Maybe. A key insight of welfare economics is that one inefficient policy *can* counter-act another inefficient policy. But does this insight apply in this particular case? Let's work through matters step by step.

First, imagine laissez-faire. There's no welfare and no minimum wage. The low-skilled labor market looks just like this:

Figure 1: Low-Skilled Labor Market Under Laissez-Faire

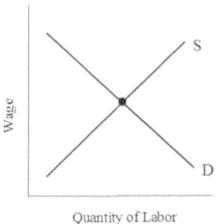

Quantity of Labor

There's no involuntary unemployment, and the big black dot reveals the wage and quantity of labor.

Now imagine adding a minimum wage – but no welfare – to the mix.

Figure 2: Low-Skilled Labor Market With Minimum Wage But No Welfare

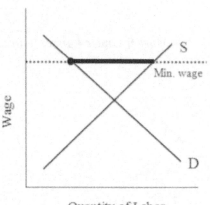

Quantity of Labor

The big black dot still reveals the wage and quantity of labor. Thanks to the minimum wage, though, there's now a lot of involuntary unemployment, marked in bold. *This is true despite the fact that the minimum wage increases the incentive to work.* Why? Because the minimum wage also reduces the incentive to hire! Since a deal only happens if *both* demanders and suppliers of labor consent, the quantity of hours worked is the *smaller* of quantity demanded and quantity supplied.

Under laissez-faire, any able-bodied worker can get a job and stand on his own two feet. The minimum wage deprives the unfortunate workers shown in bold of their ability to support themselves. Given this involuntary unemployment, the case for welfare is suddenly easier to make. What happens if the government in its mercy puts the unemployed on the dole?

Figure 3: Low-Skilled Labor Market With Minimum Wage and Welfare

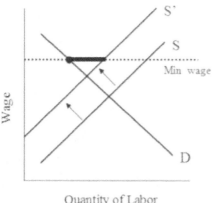

Quantity of Labor

The answer may surprise you. The supply of labor falls to S', of course, because free money makes workers less eager to work. But unless welfare is ample enough to push the market-clearing wage above the legal minimum wage, welfare has *no* effect on the wage or quantity of hours worked! Why not? *Because thanks to the minimum wage, jobs are rationed.* There's still a line of eager applicants even if the marginal payoff for work declines.

With a binding minimum wage, the only clear-cut effect of welfare is to transform *in*voluntary unemployment into voluntary unemployment. That's why the bold line shrinks: Some – though not all – of the workers who craved a job at the minimum wage now shrug, "Eh, now that I've got free money, why interview?"

On Thiel's story, though, Figure 3 doesn't fit the con-temporary labor market. He claims that welfare is now so generous that workers no longer desire minimum wage jobs. Diagrammatically:

Figure 4: Low-Skilled Labor Market With Minimum Wage and High Welfare

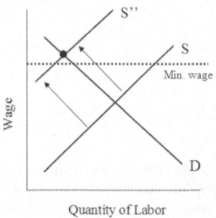

Quantity of Labor

Notice: Sufficiently high welfare makes the minimum wage irrelevant. The market now clears at the intersection of the old demand curve D and the new supply curve S". Since the intersection exceeds the minimum, the minimum has no effect. Thanks to welfare, employment is low. But whatever unemployment you see is voluntary.

OK, now we're ready to see if Thiel's story makes sense. Figure 4 roughly describes the world he thinks we're in. What would happen if, swayed by Thiel's argument, government raises the minimum wage to counteract welfare's disincentive effects?

Figure 5: Low-Skilled Labor Market With High Minimum Wage and High Welfare

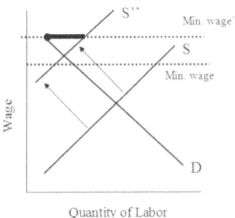

The answer, as Figure 5 clearly shows, is utterly orthodox: wages rise, employment falls, and involuntary unemployment revives. How is this possible? Simple. Generous welfare benefits do nothing to vitiate the truism that the minimum wage simultaneously raises the incentive to *work* and cuts the incentive to *hire*. And as usual, a deal only happens if *both* demanders and suppliers consent. The market therefore goes to the intersection of quantity demanded and the new minimum wage, with unemployment shown in bold.

The lesson: When the minimum wage causes involuntary unemployment, raising welfare can serve as a band-aid for the labor market. Workers deprived of the right to provide for themselves can subsist on government money. Yet when welfare convinces people to abandon honest toil, raising the minimum wage is *no* band-aid. Instead, raising the minimum wage salts the wounds. The reason, to repeat: While a higher minimum wage does indeed make workers more eager to work, it also automatically makes employers less eager to hire.

I have great respect for Peter Thiel, but his concession to minimum wage advocates is confused. While some inefficient policies can offset the effects of other inefficient policies, the minimum wage is not such a policy. It doesn't matter if welfare is high, low, or non-existent. The minimum wage causes unemployment by making marginal workers unprofitable to employ.

February 24, 2014

* * *

Notes

1. Marinucci, Carla. "Billionaire Tech Star Peter Thiel, Big GOP Donor, Says Time to 'Seriously Consider' $12/Hr Minimum Wage." *SFGate* (blog), February 21, 2014.

Health Insurance, Fairness Norms, and Unemployment

Nominal wages rarely fall – even when there's high unemployment. Part of the reason is regulation, of course. But even under laissez-faire, employers have to cope with human psychology. Almost all workers think that nominal wages cuts are unfair. And while employers might be tempted to say, "Fairness be damned," they have to face the fact that hurting worker morale hurts productivity and profits.

So how can the market get back to equilibrium? The simplest solution is to freeze nominal wages and wait for inflation to bring the real wage back to realistic levels. A more proactive solution, though, is to cut *benefits*, and hope workers don't mind.

Cutting benefits sounds crafty. But on reflection, it might be even worse than cutting wages. Consider: Most workers' main benefit is health insurance. If employers curtailed this benefit, would workers find it unfair? I don't know of any survey research on this point, but I'll bet that most workers would react *viscerally* to cuts in health insurance. Higher co-payments? Unfair! Tighter coverage? Unfair! Cheaper plan? Unfair, unfair, unfair!

It gets worse. Unlike wages, health insurance costs go up *automatically* – at a rate well above inflation. So even in the midst of severe unemployment, total nominal labor costs keep rising – unless employers choose to risk severe morale problems.

In past recessions, this was probably a small effect. Back in 1980, health care was only 9.2% of GDP. By 2009, this percentage had nearly doubled to 17.6%. To get a feel for the numbers, consider George Mason. My total Kaiser premium is $1448 per month. If this rises 5% per year, labor costs soar $2700 in just three years. Relative to an econ professor's salary, that's not much. But for lower-paid workers, it's huge. Even if there were a "total pay freeze," a worker who cost $30k in 2008 would cost 9% more in 2011.

My speculation: The high and rising cost of health insurance, combined with health insurance fairness norms, is a major reason why employment is recovering so slowly. If I'm right, we've got a serious problem with no easy solution. As always, though, we should start with the low-hanging fruit: Don't mandate coverage, don't punish firms for trying to control costs, and above all, don't amplify workers' dysfunctional beliefs about fairness with demagoguery.[1] Sigh.

August 23, 2011

* * *

Notes

1. Caplan, Bryan. "A Closer Look at Adverse Selection and Mandatory Insurance." *EconLog*, July 1, 2009.

The Joy of Market-Clearing Wages

When people compare the U.S. and Europe, they often conclude that the U.S. is richer and more economically efficient, but that Europe is happier because they don't measure everything in dollars and cents (or even Marks and Pfennigs). One of the prime examples people often point to: America's less regulated, more flexible labor markets versus Europe's highly regulated, highly rigid labor markets. (Exceptions: The UK and Holland). The U.S. sure looks more efficient, but many think of the European system as more humane.

There is a broad consensus among economists that European-style labor market regs are the main reason why European unemployment is so much higher than that in the U.S. Everyone from me to Paul Krugman agrees.

Still, you might argue that the European approach makes people happier. There is some increased risk of unemployment, but workers get higher earnings. If labor demand is inelastic, it seems like this could make most people better off. (Even this needs lots of qualifications, but I'll buy it for the sake of argument).

So what? Well, if you delve into the life satisfaction literature, you learn two fun facts.

1. Once you reach a modest standard of living, additional income does not increase life satisfaction very much. Marginal utility of wealth decreases rapidly – maybe even more rapidly than you thought. (Having been a happy grad student on $6000/year, it's not more rapid than *I* thought).

2. Unemployment *per se* has a large effect on life satisfaction. If you compare two people with equal incomes, one employed, one unemployed, the unemployed one is typically a lot less happy.

Just to get a feel for these results, Donovan and Halpern report (Chart 11) that about 80% of people in almost every occupational category is "fairly" or "very" satisfied with their lives.[1] Manual laborers and white-collar workers are nearly equal in satisfaction. Managers are a bit higher, around 90%. But the unemployed are fully 20 percentage points less likely than most workers to be satisfied with their lives.

Suppose, then, that labor market regulation could raise the incomes of manual laborers up to the level of white-collar workers. That's a big change, but the extra income would probably add at most 1 percentage point of life satisfaction. If a side effect of the regulation was increasing the unemployment rate by 5%, however, this gain would be exactly balanced by the decreased satisfaction of the unemployed. And this is true even if we ignore all of the other side effects of the regulation – from extra taxes to pay for extra workers on the dole, to higher prices from restricted supply.

If you think this is remotely accurate, you will flee in terror from any regulation that might marginally push up unemployment. Flexible labor markets are more than just efficient. Contrary to popular prejudice, they also make a lot of people happy by making it easy to find a job.

April 1, 2005

* * *

Notes

1. Donovan, N., D. Halpern, R. Sargeant, and Great Britain Prime Minister's Strategy Unit. *Life Satisfaction: The State of Knowledge and Implications for Government.* Cabinet Office, Strategy Unit, 2002.

Part II

Open Borders

Economism and Immigration

In our immigration debate, Mark Krikorian heavily downplayed the relevance of economic arguments.[1] Instead of focusing on immigration's economic benefits, we should dwell on the damage immigration does to our national solidarity, culture, and politics. His reply to my post-debate questions underscores this point.[2] Rather than challenge the astronomical estimates of the economic benefits of open borders, Mark repeats, "And immigration policy isn't purely an economic matter in any case."

But if immigrants have such baleful non-economic effects, why don't natives protect themselves by moving to low-immigration regions of the country? Mark suddenly sings a different tune: "Both natives and immigrants will go where the jobs are."

Reconciling Mark's two claims is not easy. If the non-economic effects of immigration are so important, why would natives primarily base their locational decisions on economic factors? Yes, you *could* say, "Public policy should be based on immigration's non-economic effects, even though private choices largely ignore these effects." But it's a bizarre position. When people can escape genuine social ills by moving, they usually move.

The intellectually cleanest objection is that all the important harm of immigration happens at the *national* level, so moving to another part of the country is useless. But this is silly. Whatever you think about the overall effects of immigration, these effects are clearly far more *pronounced* in California, New York, and Texas than they are in West Virginia, North Dakota, and Nebraska.

What's the logical inference? The absence of a native exodus to low-immigration states reveals some mixture of the following:

1. Natives don't actually care that much about immigrants' non-economic effects; their complaining is nationalist cheap talk driven by Social Desirability Bias.[3]

2. The non-economic effects of immigration are neutral or good.

The beauty of locational decisions, moreover, is that you can make them unilaterally. If no one but anti-immigration activists appreciates the true value of unsullied American culture, they don't have to change multicultural minds to find a better life for themselves. The activists only have to change their own addresses. So why don't they? This is especially clear for activists who own homes in California, New York, or DC; they really can escape most of the horrors of immigration and miniaturize their mortgages in one fell swoop.[4]

P.S. Good for you if you're already asking yourself, "If libertarian policies are so great, why don't people move to the freest states?" The quick answer is, "They do."[5]

May 26, 2014

* * *

Notes

1. YouTube. "Should America Open Its Borders? Reason Presents a Debate on Immigration," May 11, 2014.
2. Caplan, Bryan. "Talking More to Mark Krikorian." *EconLog*, May 23, 2014.
3. Caplan, Bryan. "Demagoguery Explained." *EconLog*, May 3, 2014.
4. Caplan, Bryan. "Million Dollar Babies: Economic Fact versus Popular Fancy in L.A." *EconLog*, January 6, 2007.
5. Ruger, William, and Jason Sorens. *Freedom in the 50 States: An Index of Personal and Economic Freedom.* Fourth edition. Washington, D.C: Cato Institute, 2016.

Market Forces vs. Discrimination: What We Learn from Illegal Immigration

Illegal immigrants are one of the few groups that modern Americans openly despise. Indeed, most people can't even say "illegal immigrants" without sneer italics. Illegal immigrants are also one of the few groups that effectively can't sue their employers for discrimination; if they make a stink, they get deported before they get to trial. The upshot: If *anyone* nowadays suffers from labor market discrimination, it's illegal immigrants.

But notice: Americans have zero confidence in the ability of *legal* discrimination against this *hated* group to "protect their jobs from illegals" or discourage border crossing in the first place. No, they think American employers are far too greedy to pass up this golden opportunity to hire on the cheap.

In other words, it looks like most Americans already implicitly accept the Beckerian thoughtcrime that market forces alone heavily discourage – and ultimately eliminate – discrimination. Not for minorities, women, or gays of course; there Americans imagine that regulation and lawsuits explain virtually all progress since 1950. But for discrimination against the most despised minority of all, illegal immigrants, Americans firmly believe that greed trumps prejudice. And that's why discrimination against illegals isn't just legally allowed, but required.

November 30, 2010

Immigration and Wages: A Socratic Dialogue

Glaucon: You're an economist, right?

    Socrates: Yes, I was recently promoted from philosopher to philosopher-economist.

Glaucon: You agree, then, that increasing supply reduces prices.

Socrates: All else equal, yes.

Glaucon: Well, I've heard some "economists" claim that immigration might actually *increase* native wages.[1]

Socrates: You've heard correctly.

Glaucon: I can see how immigration might raise the wages of *some* natives. If the immigrants need housing, for example, native construction workers might benefit from the increase in demand. But immigration couldn't increase native wages in general.

Socrates: Why not?

Glaucon: Standard labor economics says that labor demand depends entirely on workers' marginal productivity.

Socrates: Indeed.

Glaucon: Well, the most immigration can do is shift labor demand around. It doesn't actually raise natives' productivity. How could it?

Socrates: Perhaps immigration encourages natives to specialize in jobs where they are especially productive – and subcontract their other jobs to the new arrivals.

Glaucon: Huh? How can you equate specialization and trade with "raising productivity"? Sophistry!

Socrates: Perhaps. Would you mind helping me to clarify my thinking, dear Glaucon?

Glaucon: Well, I guess I've got nothing better to do.

Socrates: Very well then. Suppose a man finds a tool. Would you call it "sophistry" to say that this tool raises the man's productivity?

Glaucon: No. What could be clearer?

Socrates: What if someone claimed that it was the *tool*, not the man, who was more productive than before?

Glaucon: He's splitting hairs. Men with tools produce more stuff than men without tools. Therefore tools make men more productive.

Socrates: I see. What would you say, then, if a man domesticated an animal? Would you call it "sophistry" to say that the animal raises the man's productivity?

Glaucon: Mmm... no. Economically speaking, an animal is merely a living tool.

Socrates: What if the man had to entice the animal to work with treats? Would that change anything?

Glaucon: Not a thing. Economically speaking, giving an animal treats to make it work harder is no different than polishing a tool to make it sharper.

Socrates: Very well. Now I ask you: What if the animal is *a man from another land*?

Glaucon: What?!

Socrates: I repeat: What if the animal is *a man from another* *land?*

Glaucon: How can you compare the two?

Socrates: How can you dispute the comparison? You admit that a tool raises workers' productivity. You admit that an animal is a tool. Do you deny that humans are animals? Or that immigrants are human?

Glaucon: You're being ridiculous. Animals are useful tools because they are *better* than humans at certain tasks. Low-skilled immigrants are worse than natives at everything.

Socrates: "Everything" seems too strong. But suppose you're right: Natives are more productive than immigrants at everything. Does this preclude mutually profitable trade between natives and immigrants?

Glaucon: You're reminding me of an international trade class.

Socrates: Indeed. In your trade class, you almost certainly learned about the Law of Comparative Advantage.[2] Mutually beneficial trade is possible even if one country has an absolute advantage in *everything*.

Glaucon: I see where you're headed. You're going to say that free trade is mutually beneficial, and immigration is just free trade in labor, so immigration is mutually beneficial. You know what? I'm just going to deny the premise. Free trade *doesn't* benefit natives workers.

Socrates: Please go on.

Glaucon: I'd be delighted. I'm just generalizing my original argument. Wages depend on productivity, and trade doesn't magically make native workers more productive.

Socrates: Strangely, Glaucon, I believe in the magic you deny.

Glaucon: Guffaw!

Socrates: Perhaps you're right, but let me tell you a little fable about the magic I believe in. Once upon a time, a businessman announced to the world that he knew how to turn corn into cars.

Glaucon: More magic!

Socrates: That's exactly what the scientists in my fable say. But lo and behold, the businessman builds a factory by the ocean. Tons of corn disappear inside his factory, and thousands of cars emerge. Everyone's baffled, but they like his cars.

Glaucon: Socrates, I'm out of patience.

Socrates: Fear not, I'm nearly finished. Hypothetically speaking, do you admit that this factory, if it existed, would have genuinely raised worker productivity?

Glaucon: Get to the point.

Socrates: Very well. One day, a journalist sneaks into the factory and discovers that there's no machinery inside. Just ships. The businessman's recipe for turning corn into cars is: export corn, import cars.

Glaucon: So his "magic" was fraudulent.

Socrates: Why "fraudulent"? I say his magic was real. Economically speaking, the businessman *did* figure out how to turn corn into cars – and his workers became more productive as a result. Do you deny this?

Glaucon: I suppose not. But we've strayed so far from our original debate, and have so little to show for it, that I wish I'd never started our conversation.

Socrates: Perhaps my reflections were fruitless, Glaucon, but yours were not. Ten minutes ago you told me, "Wages depend on productivity, and trade doesn't magically make native workers more productive." Now you seem to believe in the magic of trade as firmly as I do.

Glaucon: It still seems like sophistry. Of what use are a bunch of low-skilled immigrants?

Socrates: I suspect you find uses for them every day. Low-skilled immigrants pick your vegetables, prepare your meals, mow your lawn, watch your kids, and help your aged parents. You *could* do all these tasks yourself, but you choose not to. May I ask why?

Glaucon: I'm just too busy.

Socrates: Or in other words, without "a bunch of low-skilled immigrants," you would be less productive. Call it magic. Call it economics. Either way, it's real. For all practical purposes, low-skilled immigrants raise the productivity of native workers. And as far as supply and demand is concerned, it's entirely possible for immigrants to actually boost natives' wages.

October 4, 2010

* * *

Notes

1. Caplan, Bryan. "Immigration Restrictions: A Solution in Search of a Problem." *EconLog*, September 17, 2010.
2. Caplan, Bryan. "Where Eugenics Goes Wrong: The Implications of Comparative Advantage." *EconLog*, January 21, 2006.

National Origin as Nurture Effect

Abundant adoption and twin studies find minimal long-run nurture effects.[1] In plain language: The family that raises you has little effect on your adult outcomes. A key caveat, though, is that almost all of these studies come from the First World.[2] Does growing up elsewhere durably stunt personal development? Existing evidence is largely silent.

While reading the National Academy of Sciences all-new report on *The Economic and Fiscal Consequences of Immigration*, though, I finally encountered some relevant data – though unfortunately, it only allows us to measure the effect of growing up in the U.S. versus *anywhere* else.[3]

Background: To estimate an immigrant's long-run fiscal effect, you must also estimate how successful his descendants will be. The NAS explains its method:

> In order to forecast taxes and benefits for an average immigrant and descendants, it is necessary to first forecast the ultimate educational attainment for young immigrants and the future educational attainment of the offspring of immigrants. The panel predicted the education of offspring as a func-

tion of parental education using regression analysis based on CPS samples 15 years apart... Adult child education is regressed on parental education by birth region, with separate equations for native-born children versus foreign-born children. This generates equations that are used to predict a child's ultimate educational attainment...

Big finding: Children of immigrants have *markedly* greater educational success than you would expect given their foreign-born parent's education. While children always tend to resemble their parents, the resemblance is stronger when both child and parent are native-born.

Estimates for children of natives:

Parent's Education	Child's Education				
	Less Than High School	High School Graduate	Some College	Bachelor's Degree	More Than Bachelor's Degree
1. Less than high school	29.4	50.9	18.4	1.3	0.0
2. High school graduate	7.6	42.2	42.2	7.8	0.2
3. Some college	1.0	16.9	50.1	28.8	3.2
4. Bachelor's degree	0.0	2.3	26.0	51.8	19.9
5. More than bachelor's degree	0.0	0.3	7.0	40.3	52.4

Estimates for children of immigrants:

Parent's Education	Child's Education				
	Less Than High School	High School Graduate	Some College	Bachelor's Degree	More Than Bachelor's Degree
1. Less than high school	17.1	44.1	32.4	6.2	0.3
2. High school graduate	4.3	27.2	46.2	20.3	2.0
3. Some college	0.7	11.9	40.2	38.0	9.2
4. Bachelor's degree	0.1	2.2	21.7	46.5	29.5
5. More than bachelor's degree	0.0	0.6	8.8	37.7	52.9

The most striking achievement gaps: Less than 20% of

children of native-born high school dropouts go beyond high school, but almost *40%* of children of foreign-born high school dropouts pass this milestone. Similarly, about half of children of native-born high school grads surpass their parents' attainment – versus over *two-thirds* of children of immigrant high school grads.

What does this teach us about the power of nurture? For the sake of argument, assume that everyone born in the United States enjoys the same educational environment, so genes (and luck) explain all remaining disparities.* Then we can use immigrants' *children's* success to measure the stunting effect of growing up *outside* the United States! Intuitively: *If a native and an immigrant's children perform equally well, we should infer that their parents had equal genetic potential.*

For convenience, let's code the five educational categories as continuous variables: less than high school =1, high school graduate =2, some college =3, bachelor's degree =4, more than bachelor's =5. Then here is children's average educational attainment E, conditional on their parents':

	Expected Child's Education (E)	
Parental Education	Native Parent	Immigrant Parent
1	1.9	2.3
2	2.5	2.9
3	3.2	3.4
4	3.9	4.0
5	4.4	4.4

We can use this information to construct another table mapping immigrants' observed education into their *potential* education – i.e., the education they would have acquired if they'd been born in the United States. Example: The American-born children of immigrants who didn't finish high school ($E=1$) have average attainment $E=2.3$. That's two-thirds of the way between kids of natives who didn't finish high school ($E=1.9$) and kids of natives who finished high school ($E=2.5$). In other words, immigrants with $E=1$ have the kids you'd *expect* from parents with $E=1.67$! Filling in the rest of the table:

Immigrant Education		Environmental Deprivation
Actual	Potential	
1	1.67	-0.67
2	2.57	-0.57
3	3.29	-0.29
4	4.20	-0.20
5	5.00	0.00

Now we're ready to calculate the nurture effects of national origin. There's no harm at the tip-top: Non-Americans with advanced degrees look intrinsically no abler than Americans with advanced degrees. As you move down the educational ladder, however, environmental deprivation goes from moderate (-.20 steps for college grads) to serious (-.57 steps for high school grads, -.67 for less than high school). And if you think that American-born children of immigrant parents are also somewhat deprived, their parents' estimated environmental deprivation is even worse.

Main doubt: The NAS correlates success for *individual* parents and their kids. In principle, then, kids of immigrants could have one native-born parent – and kids of native-born parents could have one immigrant parent. Ideally, we'd compare kids of two immigrant parents to kids of two native parents. Given the strong correlation in spousal education, though, this probably *understates* immigrants' deprivation.[4] Genetically speaking, an immigrant who marries an equally-educated native is "marrying down."

The implications for immigration are debatable.[5] So are the implications for education.[6] But the implications for nurture effects are clear.[7] If you grew up in a *relatively* deprived American home, adoption and twin research imply that your educational success would have barely changed. If you grew up in an *absolutely* deprived *non*-American home, however, your educational success would have been markedly worse – masking your underlying genetic potential.[8] The broader but still provisional lesson: Nurture matters after all. Behavioral geneticists have struggled to detect nurture effects because of range restriction – not because there's nothing to detect.

* Whether or not you buy this assumption, it still sets a lower bound on nurture effects. Keep reading.

December 15, 2016

* * *

Notes

1. Caplan, Bryan. *Selfish Reasons to Have More Kids: Why Being a Great Parent Is Less Work and More Fun than You Think.* New York: Basic Books, 2011.
2. Caplan, Bryan. "Dude, Where's My Theory of Everything?" *EconLog*, February 21, 2011.
3. National Academies of Sciences, Engineering, and Medicine (U.S.), Francine Blau, Christopher Mackie, National Academies of Sciences, Engineering, and Medicine (U.S.), and National Academies of Sciences, Engineering, and Medicine (U.S.), eds. *The Economic and Fiscal Consequences of Immigration.* Washington, D.C: National Academies Press, 2017.
4. Caplan, Bryan. "Ballparking the Marital Return to College." *EconLog*, February 18, 2014.
5. Caplan, Bryan. "A Swarm of Thoughts on Hive Mind." *EconLog*, November 18, 2015.
6. Caplan, Bryan. "International Evidence on the Human Capital/Signaling Split." *EconLog*, October 7, 2013.
7. Caplan, Bryan. "A Conversation With Judy Harris." *EconLog*, April 1, 2009.
8. Caplan, Bryan. "A Swarm of Thoughts on Hive Mind." *EconLog*, November 18, 2015.

The Diversity Lottery: Some Rough Open Borders Arithmetic

How many people want to immigrate to the U.S.? In my past work, I've appealed to both surveys and black market prices to ballpark the answer.[1] Another approach, however, is to take a look at the U.S. Diversity lottery. Every year, the U.S. takes applications from would-be immigrants all over the world. Countries like Mexico, China, and India that already send lots of immigrants to the U.S. are excluded. Further requirements:

> If selected, to qualify for the immigrant visa, they must have completed at least a high school education or at least two years of work experience in an occupation which requires at least two other years of training or experience. They must also satisfy general immigration requirements, such as means of support, no criminal background, and good health.

The lottery has roughly 125,000 "finalists" and 50,000 actual slots.[*2] Finalists are invited to apply for a green card, but optimistically only half of applicants actually get the visa. This implies that about 100,000 out of the 125,000 finalists apply –

about 80%.

Since this is an actual lottery, we can plausibly infer that 80% of *all* applicants would come if they won. In 2018, there were about 15M applications for a total of 23M would-be immigrants. If they were all admitted, that comes to 18.4M immigrants *per year*. In 2018, non-lottery immigration was roughly 1M.

Does this mean that open borders would multiply immigration roughly by a factor of 20? That's too simple, but complications go in both directions. An immigrant flow that large might lead to short-run labor market disruptions large enough to keep some would-be immigrants at home. Similarly, if immigration were that high, U.S.-based relatives would be less willing and able to help new arrivals get on their feet. This, too, would deter migration. Note: Even if these effects are initially mild, they would likely build over time. One year of 20M migrants might not hurt a would-be immigrant's labor prospects too much, but five years in a row of such immigration probably would.

Furthermore, current Diversity lottery applicants are probably *highly* motivated to move to the U.S. A few years of open borders would allow all highly-motivated would-be migrants to come, leading to lower subsequent migration in equilibrium.

On the other hand, however, *many* millions of would-be immigrants currently fail to enter the Diversity lottery because (a) they've never heard of it; (b) the odds seem hopelessly low; (c) people hate filling out paperwork; (d) they don't want to separate from their families; (e) they're from an ineligible country; or (f) they lack the required education or experience.[3] Open borders would drastically mitigate all six problems.

Which factors would dominate? I honestly don't know. Yet if we're only trying to ballpark immigration under open borders, 20M a year is not a bad guess.

* Officially, there are 55,000 slots, but 5000 have been diverted to the NACARA program.

July 20, 2020

* * *

Notes

1. Ray, Julie, Neli Esipova, and Anita Pugliese. "More Than 750 Million Worldwide Would Migrate If They Could." *Gallup,* December 10, 2018.; Caplan, Bryan. "Why Is Illegal Immigration So Low?" *EconLog,* June 4, 2015.
2. Probasco, Jim. "How the Green Card Lottery Really Works." *Investopedia*, n.d.
3. Caplan, Bryan. "The Behavioral Econ of Paperwork." *EconLog*, May 23, 2017.

Why Is Illegal Immigration So Low?

C ontrary to popular opinion, U.S. immigration enforcement is draconian. The proof is in the prices illegal immigrants pay to human smugglers. Even Mexicans, our closest Third World neighbors, pay 2-3 *years'* worth of wages to illegally cross the border.[1] Every other Third World nationality pays more. Millions of immigrants come illegally not because the cost is low but because the benefits are high.

Even so, observed levels of immigration are puzzlingly low.[2] Let's stick with Mexico for simplicity. $3000 is a lot for a Mexican farmworker *in Mexico*, but not so much for a Mexican farmworker in the U.S. Suppose annual farm pay in Mexico is $1500, versus $15,000 in the U.S. That's a raise of $13,500 a year. Once he arrives, a Mexican worker could recoup his smuggling fee in under 12 weeks. Why then do most stay home?

True, these numbers ignore the horrors of the border crossing. They are bad, but still seem modest compared to the magnitude of the gain. A 0.1% risk of death is a pretty high estimate.[3] According to standard calculations, pampered Americans would only pay $7000 or so to avoid that risk. For would-be Mexican immigrants, even $1000 seems high.

Another major flaw in these calculations is that they assume that paying a human smuggler gets you into the U.S. for sure. In reality, the success rate is around 50%.[4] The *expected* cost of crossing into the United States is therefore roughly double what it seems.

But neither of these sensible adjustments do much to resolve the puzzle. Add $1000 danger cost to the $3000 out-of-pocket cost. Then divide the sum by the probability of successful crossing. It implies that, on average, Mexicans recoup their full smuggling costs in 31 weeks. That's still a great return on investment – 167% per year.

What other factors are at work? One story I've heard is that illegal immigrants' *expected* gain is much lower than it seems because they only earn American wages if *employed.* But this seems a trivial factor. Illegal immigrants' unemployment risk is only slightly higher than natives'.[5] And don't forget there's unemployment risk back in Mexico, too.

George Borjas suggests that people's strong attachment to their homeland deters migration. He's right about the general phenomenon, but grossly exaggerates the magnitude.[6] In any case, feelings of attachment vary widely, and current immigration is far below potential. So you would still expect the *marginal* illegal immigrant's attachment to Mexico to be mild, leaving the puzzle intact.

The key factor, in my view, is quite different: *Illegal immigration is relatively low because would-be immigrants have crummy credit and insurance options.*

1. *Crummy credit options.* Most rural Mexicans can't just go to the bank to get an illegal immigration loan. Nor can they pay a coyote with a credit card. They start in a desperate situation

with a lousy credit rating. To cross the border, they have to save *years'* worth of their own income, borrow years' worth of income from similarly desperate relatives and friends, or pay frighteningly high black market rates. When economists invoke such arguments to explain Americans' behavior, I'm skeptical. For poor people in developing countries, though, credit constraints are clearly a big deal.

What behavior economists call "debt aversion" amplifies the credit problem. Most human beings dislike "being in debt," even when the debt quickly pays for itself.

2. *Crummy insurance options.* Rural Mexicans can't readily buy "illegal immigration insurance." So when they finally accumulate their nest egg to cross the border, they're risking their life savings. 50% chance of crossing the border and entering the land of plenty, 50% of losing their nest egg and getting sent back to Mexico. A terrifying gamble. The black market could offer such insurance, of course, but would-be customers are right to worry they'll never get to collect.

Various choice-under-uncertainty anomalies probably amplify the insurance problem.

And that's the heart of my story. In a free market, of course, poor Mexicans would have access to reputable international lenders and insurers. But neither the U.S. nor the Mexican government would tolerate major First World corporations financing illegal migration.

I hope no one will mistake my analytical approach for lack of sympathy with illegal immigrants' plight. In a just world, they could enter the land of opportunity for the price of a bus ticket.[7] My point is that relatively low levels of immigration do *not* show that the seemingly immense gains of border crossing are illusory. The gains are genuine. They're just hard for people in desperate poverty to realize with only the black market to help them.

HT: Partly inspired by a Facebook exchange with Bill Dickens, and Alex Nowrasteh's request.[8]

June 4, 2015

* * *

Notes

1. Caplan, Bryan. "The Behavioral Econ of Paperwork." *EconLog*, May 23, 2017.
2. Nowrasteh, Alex. "Why Are There So Few Unlawful Immigrants?" Cato Institute, June 4, 2013.
3. "Migrant deaths along the Mexico–United States border," *Wikipedia*.
4. Plumer, Brad. "Study: The U.S. Stops about Half of Illegal Border Crossings from Mexico - The Washington Post." *The Washington Post*, May 13, 2013.
5. Passel, Jeffrey, and D'Vera Cohn. "U.S. Unauthorized Immigration Flows Are Down Sharply Since Mid-Decade." Pew Research Center's Hispanic Trends Project, September 1, 2010.
6. Caplan, Bryan. "Trillion Dollar Bills on the Sidewalk: The Borjas Critique." *EconLog*, July 16, 2014.
7. Huemer, Michael. "Is There a Right to Immigrate?" *Social Theory and Practice* 36, no. 3 (July 2010): 429–261.
8. Nowrasteh, Alex. "Response to Bryan Caplan." Cato

Institute, June 3, 2015.

Trillion-Dollar Bills on the Sidewalk: The Borjas Critique

George Borjas' new *Immigration Economics* contains the first intellectually serious critique of the increasingly mainstream view that open borders are a big stack of "trillion-dollar bills on the sidewalk."[1] Borjas begins by clearly explaining what's at stake.

> [W]hat types of gains would accrue to the world's population if countries suddenly decided to remove all legal restraints to international migration and workers moved to those countries that afforded them the best economic opportunities? In contrast to the immigration surplus calculated for the receiving country's native population in the previous sections, it turns out that the "global immigration surplus" is huge and seemingly could do away with much of world poverty in one fell swoop.[2]

The critical variable is R, the First World/Third World wage ratio for equally-skilled labor:

> As in the original Hamilton-Whalley (1984) study,

the exercise reveals that the gains to world income are huge. If R=2, for example, world GDP would rise by $9.4 trillion, a 13.4 percent increase over the initial value of $70 trillion. If R=4, world GDP would increase by $40 trillion, almost a 60 percent increase. In fact, if R were to equal 6, which may be near the upper bound of the range of plausibility suggested by the available data, world GDP would rise by $62 trillion, a near-doubling. Note, moreover, that these gains would be accrued each year after the migration occurs, so that the present value of the gains would be astronomically high.

The Borjas critique:

Even putting aside the political difficulties in enacting such a policy [open borders], this argument in favor of unrestricted international migration glosses over two conceptual obstacles.

First, the calculation assumes that people can somehow start at a specific latitude-longitude coordinate and end up at a different coordinate at *zero cost*... The absence of legal restrictions prohibiting the movement of people from one country to another does not circumvent the fact that it would be very costly to move billions of workers.

As noted in chapter 1, large wage differences across regions can persist for a very long time simply because *many people choose not to move*. In a world of income-maximizing agents, the stayers are signaling that there are substantial psychic costs to mobility, perhaps on the order of hundreds of thousands [sic] dollars per person... Kennan and Walker (2011 p.232) for instance, estimate that it costs $312,000 to move the average person from one state to another within the United States...

Although these costs seem implausibly high, moving costs must be around this order of magnitude to account for the observed fact that people do not move as much as they should given the existing regional wage differences. If moving costs were indeed in that range, it is easy to show that the huge global gains from migration become substantially smaller and may even vanish after taking moving costs into account. [emphasis original]

Borjas then does some back-of-the-envelope calculations and concludes:

The "breakeven" cost of migration given in the last row of Table 7.3 is around $140,000. In short, the entire present value of the global gains is wiped out even if the costs of migration were only half of what is typically reported in existing studies.

Qualitatively, Borjas' argument is entirely true. Human welfare rises by less than GDP because of material and psychic relocation costs. But quantitatively, Borjas' argument is ludicrous. Yes, he's seriously using the *average* valuations of *Americans* to estimate the *marginal* valuations of *Third Worlders*! Yet any decent econ undergrad can tell you that:

1. The marginal migrant minds moving less than average. Indeed, given the strictness of the current regime, many marginal migrants would probably take a wage *cut* to exit their homelands. Think of every Iraqi Shiite who can't sleep tonight because the Sunnis are coming, and every Iraqi Sunni who can't sleep tonight because the Shiites are coming.

2. Third Worlders are almost certainly willing to pay vastly less than Americans to stay in their homelands because *location is a normal good*. Indeed, location is probably a luxury. Does Borjas really think that most Haitians would forego $140,000 in income because they're in love with Port-au-Prince?

An excellent econ undergrad might add that:

3. Due to diaspora dynamics, psychic relocation costs endogenously fall over time.[3] The more migrants there are, the easier it is to say adios to your country of birth. Forget Maine, but remember Puerto Rico.[4]

Points #1 and #2 are so basic that I reviewed all of Borjas' attendant footnotes to see if he addresses them. He grudgingly accedes to #1 in footnote 22:

> Only a subset of persons in the data are actually observed to move, so that the subsample of movers may have moving costs that differ substantially from (and may be much lower than) the "average" estimates for hypothetical movers.

But to the best of my knowledge, Borjas never even hints at #2 – a bizarre omission given his childhood flight from Cuba. He does however further undercut his critique in footnote 20:

It is worth noting that a disproportionately large fraction of the global gains can be accrued even if only a fraction of the potential movers migrate to the North. For example, global GDP would increase by around 17 percent when 10 percent of the potential movers move (assuming R=4).

At this point, you may be asking, "Wait, didn't Borjas promise us *two* 'conceptual obstacles'?" He did. Sadly, his second is a throwaway objection with a single citation.

[T]he gains reported in Table 7.3 depend crucially on the assumption that the intercepts of the labor demand curves in the North and South are fixed. However, the North's demand curve lies above the South's demand curve, not simply because that is just the way things are, but because of very specific political, economic, institutional, and cultural factors that endogenously led to the development of different infrastructures in the two regions...

As the important work of Acemoglu and Robinson (2012) suggests, "nations fail" mainly because of differences in political and economic institutions. For immigration to generate substantial global gains, it must be the case that billions of immigrants can move to the industrialized economies without importing the "bad" institutions that led to poor economic conditions in the source countries in the first place. It seems inconceivable that the North's infrastructure would remain unchanged after the admission of billions of new workers.

> Unfortunately, remarkably little is known about the political and cultural impact of immigration on the receiving countries, and about how institutions in these receiving countries would adjust to the influx.

That's all Borjas has to offer. Is he really unaware that plenty of research on the political consequences of immigration is already out there? (See Gochenour and Nowrasteh's literature review for starters.)[5] Is it really so difficult to picture major mitigating and countervailing factors?[6] And why would one of the world's foremost immigration scholars bemoan our "unfortunate" ignorance of "the political and cultural impact of immigration on the receiving countries" instead of rolling up his sleeves and investigating the issue? Yes, we all have a limited time budget, but isn't the prospect of "doing away with much of world poverty in one fell swoop" slightly more pressing than, say, measuring the effect of migrant Soviet mathematicians on academic mathematics?[7]

To be blunt, I suspect that Borjas *prefers* to remain agnostic about the political and cultural effects of immigration. That way, no matter how mighty the economic case for open borders, he'll never have to say, "Good God, how could I have been so blind? There's a whole stack of trillion-dollar bills right there on the sidewalk!"

July 16, 2014

* * *

Notes

1. Borjas, George. *Immigration Economics*. Cambridge, Massachusetts: Harvard University Press, 2014.

2. Clemens, Michael A. "Economics and Emigration: Trillion-Dollar Bills on the Sidewalk?" *Journal of Economic Perspectives* 25, no. 3 (August 1, 2011): 83–106.

3. Caplan, Bryan. "Diasporas, Swamping, and Open Borders Abolitionism." *EconLog*, February 5, 2014.

4. Caplan, Bryan. "The Swamping That Wasn't: The Diaspora Dynamics of the Puerto Rican Open Borders Experiment." *EconLog*, March 27, 2014.

5. Gochenour, Zachary, and Alex Nowrasteh. "The Political Externalities of Immigration: Evidence from the United States." Cato Institute Working Paper #14, January 15, 2014.

6. Caplan, Bryan. "The Social and Political Realities of Immigration: A Reply to Hoste." *EconLog*, April 28, 2010.; Caplan, Bryan. "Gilens vs. the Political Externalities of Immigration." *EconLog*, September 28, 2012.

7. Borjas, George, and Kirk Doran. "The Collapse of the Soviet Union and the Productivity of American Mathematicians." *The Quarterly Journal of Economics* 127, no. 3 (August 1, 2012): 1143–1203.

Plug-and-Play People

One common complaint about proponents of open borders is that we picture human beings as interchangeable parts. If an American can do X, so can a Haitian. Why can't the open borders crowd see the obvious truth that people are *not* "plug-and-play" – that you can't jumble different kinds of people and expect them to function well together?

My instinctive reaction is to appeal to Econ 1 and basic facts.

The Econ 1: If people of different nationalities worked poorly together, employers would account for this fact in their hiring decisions. An employer with a 100% native-born American workforce would look at immigrant applicants and silently note, "Oil and water don't mix." Or perhaps he'd think, "Americans and high-caste Indians work well together, but Americans and Indian untouchables don't." Then he'd hire on the basis of these ugly truths, while paying lip service to equal opportunity and the brotherhood of man. As a result, immigrants – or at least the "wrong kind of immigrants" – would discover that migrating for better jobs is a waste of time. Jobs are better in the First World, but you have to be First-World-compatible to land one.

The basic facts: This manifestly is *not* how labor markets

work. As the opponents of immigration loudly complain, First World employers hire immigrants all the time. They eagerly hire legal immigrants – and as long as the law is laxly enforced, they furtively hire *illegal* immigrants. Even when the law criminalizes *non*-discrimination, plenty of First World employers look over their shoulders, shrug, mutter "Money's money" and break the law.[1] Doesn't this show that workers ultimately *are* plug-and-play?

Yet on reflection, my instinctive reaction misses much of the magic of the market. If you've ever been a boss, you know that getting human beings of the *same* culture to effectively cooperate together is like pulling teeth. Indeed, it's like pulling shark teeth that never stop growing back. The more different the members of your team are, the greater the miscommunication and strife.

How then do firms manage to function? The social intelligence of the leadership. Good managers know in their bones that diverse human beings *aren't* built for close cooperation. Rather than throw their hands up in despair, however, good managers rise to the challenge. True to their job description, managers *manage* their workers, forging them into effective teams *despite* their disparate abilities, personalities, and backgrounds. It's an uphill battle, and you have to keep running just to stay in place. But good managers kindle the fire of teamwork, then keep the fire burning day in, day out.

The critics of immigration are right to insist that people aren't plug-and-play. Cultural diversity definitely makes teamwork harder. Unlike the critics of immigration, however, businesses around the world treat this fact not as a plague, but a profit opportunity. Sure, some stodgy entrepreneurs mutter defeatist cliches about oil and water and keep hiring within their tribes. But more visionary entrepreneurs rise to the challenge of diversity every day. *That*'s why even the most unskilled and culturally alien workers rightly believe that the streets of the First World are paved with gold. Given half a chance, socially adept businesspeople rush to do the paving.

But isn't the workplace a relatively favorable environment for diversity? No; the opposite is true. Stores gladly open their doors to the general public because almost any human being with money to spend is a lovely customer. As long as the customers don't bite each other, the more the merrier. Landlords are a little more selective, but not much: If your credit's good and you keep the noise down to a dull roar, they'll rent to you.

Employers, in contrast, hire with trepidation. They know that co-workers need to cooperate like the fingers of a hand. One bad worker makes a whole firm look bad. One bad worker can ruin a whole day's work. One bad worker can make ten good workers quit in frustration. Outside of the army, no voluntary endeavor in modern adult life is more regimented than the workplace. Yet by the power of social intelligence, business managers make diversity run smoothly, laughing all the way to the bank.

Where does politics fit in? It's a lingering concern, but vastly overrated.[2] Most immigrants are even more politically apathetic than natives. They vote at sharply lower rates. And when they arrive in a vast new land, most of their old grievances become irrelevant overnight: Once they arrive in the U.S., Serbs and Croats, Hutus and Tutsis, even Israelis and Palestinians let bygones be bygones.[3] Political plug-and-play is unnecessary because few immigrants want to play politics in the first place.[4]

March 26, 2015

* * *

Notes

1. Caplan, Bryan. "Market Forces vs. Discrimination: What We Learn from Illegal Immigration." *EconLog*, November 30, 2010.
2. Caplan, Bryan. "The Political Externalities of Open Borders: Digest Version." *EconLog*, December 17, 2010.
3. Caplan, Bryan. "Does Conflict Immigrate?" *EconLog*, February 18, 2013.
4. Caplan, Bryan, and Vipul Naik. "A Radical Case for Open Borders." In *The Economics of Immigration*, edited by Benjamin Powell, 180–209. Oxford University Press, 2015.

The Other Cause of Immigrant Idleness

Happy Open Borders Day! The world remains light-years from free migration, but the intellectual case and elite support for open borders continue to build.[1] In honor of the day, let's explore a little topic I call … "the *other* cause of immigrant idleness."

The global poor migrate to the First World, kiss the soil, then permanently go on welfare. Idle immigrants: Nothing short of outright criminality does more to tarnish the image of immigration.[2] It smacks of ingratitude and parasitism. And while the prevalence of immigrant idleness is overstated, it is a very real problem, especially in Europe.[3]

As a cosmopolitan libertarian, my first reaction is to point fingers at the welfare state.[4] If the problem is government subsidies for indefinite idleness, the solution is to curtail not immigration, but redistribution. When the law allows it, plenty of natives permanently go on welfare, too. Rhetorically sliding from the generic evils of the welfare state to the selective evils of immigrants is effective demagoguery, but fuzzy logic.[5]

Yet on reflection, my first reaction misses a major part of the story. Countries with ample redistribution also tend to have strict labor market regulations.[6] Despite their feel-good popularity, labor market regulations have a big negative side effect: unemployment.[7]

This collateral damage is clearest for regulations that explicitly push up wages: If the law requires a 10% raise, employers can reduce the damage to their bottom line by employing fewer workers. But unless wages are perfectly flexible, *any* "pro-worker" regulation risks this disemployment effect. If the law makes employers give workers free health insurance, and workers bitterly resent offsetting pay cuts, hiring fewer workers is employers' best remaining defense.[8]

The moral: When you see an idle immigrant, you shouldn't jump to the conclusion that he's a lazy parasite. There's another possibility: Labor regulations have priced him out of a job. He's on welfare not because he doesn't want to work, but because he'd rather go on welfare than starve.

The same logic naturally holds for natives. But the concern is *especially* relevant for immigrants. The workers employers decide *not* to hire are not randomly selected. When there's a surplus of labor, employers prefer workers who definitely *won't* have linguistic or cultural issues. Workers who "need a chance to prove themselves" get hired last. Furthermore, when there's a surplus of workers, the cost of outright bigotry sharply falls.* If native employers feel a hint of antipathy for foreigners, wage floors encourage employers to act on that antipathy.[9]

All this leads to a disturbing epiphany: Labor market regulation isn't just an alternative explanation for immigrant idleness. It is a *compelling* alternative explanation because immigrants bear the brunt of labor market regulation's disemployment effect. And contrary to a few silly economists, involuntary unemployment is no vacation. It is a grave evil for jobless and society alike.[10] In fact, unemployment is an even greater social evil than it seems, because it gives xenophobia a veneer of justification.

* Why not just have two-tier wages for natives versus foreigners? Discrimination laws aside, workers resent perceived horizontal inequities, leading to disruptive morale problems.[11]

March 16, 2015

* * *

Notes

1. Caplan, Bryan. "Some Unpleasant Immigration Arithmetic." *EconLog*, November 19, 2012.; Newman, Joel. "Open Borders: The Case." *Open Borders* (blog), May 24, 2021.; Raviv, Shaun. "If People Could Immigrate Anywhere, Would Poverty Be Eliminated?" *The Atlantic*, April 26, 2013.

2. Caplan, Bryan. "Mea Culpa: How I Succumbed to Anti-Foreign Bias." *EconLog*, July 18, 2007.

3. Kerr, Sari Pekkala, and William Kerr. "Economic Impacts of Immigration: A Survey." NBER Working Paper #16736, January 2011.

4. Caplan, Bryan. "'Callous Libertarians': Missing, or Just Unfairly Maligned?" *EconLog*, March 9, 2011.

5. Caplan, Bryan. "Demagoguery Explained." *EconLog*, May 3, 2014.

6. Caplan, Bryan. "The Nuances of EU Unemployment." *EconLog*, May 27, 2009.

7. Caplan, Bryan. "The Minimum Wage vs. Welfare: Band-Aid or Salt?" *EconLog*, February 24, 2014.

8. Caplan, Bryan. "Why Don't Wages Fall During a Recession?: Q&A With Me Channeling Truman Bewley." *EconLog*, September 23, 2013.

9. Caplan, Bryan. "Market Forces vs. Discrimination: What We Learn from Illegal Immigration." *EconLog*, November 30, 2010.

10. Caplan, Bryan. "The Grave Evil of Unemployment." *EconLog*, April 23, 2013.

11. Caplan, Bryan. "Why Do Firms Prefer More Able Workers?" *EconLog*, October 22, 2013.

The Swamping that Wasn't

The best part of Collier's *Exodus* is his analysis of "diaspora dynamics."[1] In plain English, Irish like to immigrate to countries that already have a lot of Irish, Jews like to immigrate to countries that already have a lot of Jews, and Mexicans like to immigrate to countries that already have a lot of Mexicans. Collier:

> The third big thing we know [about immigration] is that the costs of migration are greatly eased by the presence in the host country of a diaspora from the country of origin. The costs of migration fall as the size of the network of immigrants who are already settled increases. So the rate of migration is determined by the width of the [income] gap, the level of income in countries of origin, and the size of the diaspora. The relationship is not additive but multiplicative: a wide gap but a small diaspora, and a small gap with with a large diaspora, will both only generate a trickle of migration. Big flows depend upon a wide gap interacting with a large diaspora and an adequate level of income in countries of origin.

I recently stumbled on an excellent example. Puerto Rico came under U.S. rule in 1898. Six years later, the U.S. Supreme Court upheld Puerto Ricans' right to freely enter the United States (*Gonzales v. Williams* [1904]).[2] Consider it open borders by judicial fiat.

Did Puerto Ricans "swamp" in? Hardly. Instead, the Supreme Court's decision sparked a century-long chain reaction. Here's the data, courtesy of historian Carmen Whalen.

TABLE 1-1. Puerto Rico's Net
Emigration, 1900–2000

Years	Net Number of Out-Migrants
1900–1910	2,000
1910–1920	11,000
1920–1930	42,000
1930–1940	18,000
1940–1950	151,000
1950–1960	470,000
1960–1970	214,000
1970–1980	65,817
1980–1990	116,571
1990–2000	130,185

Notice: When there were only a few thousand Puerto Ricans in the entire country, open borders led to only modest migration. But decade by decade (with an understandable hiatus during the Great Depression), Puerto Rican migration snowballed. In the end, you get what you'd expect from open borders: More Puerto Ricans live in America than Puerto Rico. Yet this great transformation took decades.

Not convinced? You see similar diaspora dynamics if you

break Puerto Rican immigration down by state:

TABLE 1-3. Puerto Ricans' Residence, Selected States, 1910–2000

	1910	1920	1950	1970	2000
United States: Total	1,513	11,811	301,375	1,391,463	3,406,178
Hawaii	3,510	2,581	—	—	30,005
New York	641	7,719	252,515	878,980	1,050,293
Pennsylvania	83	433	3,560	44,947	228,557
New Jersey	23	360	5,640	136,937	336,788
Illinois	23	142	3,570	88,244	157,851
Ohio	11	124	2,115	21,147	66,269
Connecticut	4	69	1,305	38,493	194,443
Massachusetts	25	163	1,175	24,561	199,207
California	342	935	10,295	46,955	140,570
Florida	83	200	4,040	29,588	482,027
Louisiana	42	217	715	1,645	7,670
Texas	14	84	1,210	4,649	69,504

Look. In 1950, there were only 4,040 Puerto Ricans in Florida – versus a quarter million in New York. Florida was far more like Puerto Rico in every way – except for the lack of Puerto Ricans. The result: The vast majority of Puerto Rican immigrants in 1950 chose to freeze in New York with their own kind than bask with the Anglos in the Florida sun. Florida eventually became Puerto Ricans' second-favorite state of residence – but only after the Puerto Rican population hit critical mass.

Since the historic 1904 Supreme Court decision, transportation costs have drastically fallen and wage gaps between the First and Third Worlds have grown. I'd expect open borders to work their magic more swiftly today than they did a century ago. But the basic point remains sound. Open borders wouldn't lead to instant "swamping." Instead, we'd see the Puerto Rican experience writ large.

March 27, 2014

* * *

Notes

1. Caplan, Bryan. "Diasporas, Swamping, and Open Borders Abolitionism." *EconLog*, February 5, 2014.
2. Findlaw. "Gonzales v. Williams." Accessed July 10, 2021.

The Other Great Shutdown

I've debated Mark Krikorian on immigration many times before, but today's crisis provides a new and gripping argument against immigration. Almost anyone can see the force of it: Coronavirus originated in China, migration brought it here, and suddenly life is terrible. Dogmatic libertarians can keep droning on about "liberty," but everyone else now plainly sees that strict immigration controls could have stopped this plague – and only strict immigration controls can stop the plagues of the future.

This argument sounds so right. What could possibly be wrong with it?

Let's start by backing up. Before the coronavirus, did we have anything close to open borders? Of course not; Mark himself has conceded this point in prior debates. Under open borders, the U.S. could easily have tens of millions of immigrants annually. A conservative estimate says that our borders are normally 95% closed. I say it's more like 98% closed.[1]

So what? Even with our borders *98% closed*, the virus had no trouble spreading here on a massive scale.[2] Once a few sick people enter your country, it spreads far and wide. The same is true all over the world. The United Kingdom is an *island nation*, but it has the second-highest body count on Earth. So it seems like we couldn't have solved our problem with moderate further restrictions; we'd need to virtually end immigration altogether. But would that be enough? No way. You would also have to virtually end international *tourism*, too. That doesn't just mean keeping foreign tourists *out*; it also means keeping domestic tourists *in*. Or at least tell your own citizens, "If you leave, you can't come back."

The upshot: Even cutting immigration down to Japanese levels would do very little about contagion. Instead, it looks like you would have to approach North Korea's policy of "no-one-gets-in-or-out-alive."

At this point, you might be wondering, "Well, couldn't we allow tourism, but simply require a strict supervised two-week quarantine for all international travelers?" Indeed you could. Sadly, this is so burdensome it would practically eliminate international tourism. Perhaps people would take one or two international trips per lifetime, spending two weeks in quarantine on arrival and return. But that's about it. The benefit of tourism is too modest to offset weeks of confinement.

Now we reach the trillion-dollar question: What *would* be enough to offset weeks of confinement? The indubitable answer is: the opportunity to permanently immigrate! If you're already willing to leave your country of birth to build a new life for yourself, two weeks of quarantine only modestly increases the cost. Even seasonal migrants would endure quarantine; they might lose a month of time on a round-trip, but U.S. agricultural wages are about five times as high as Mexico's. The punchline, then, is that if you are mortally afraid of contagion, what you need to stop is not immigration but tourism.

Which is, by the way, the opposite of what is likely to happen, because we have long been ruled by innumerate, hysterical demagogues.[3]

An immigration policy of open borders combined with a two-week quarantine would, in my view, be an immense improvement over the status quo. I'd say that would move the border from 98% closed to 95% open. If contagion were your sole objection to immigration, this is the policy you should favor.

I know, of course, that people have a long list of other objections to immigration. Indeed, as far as I recall, this is my first debate with Mark where he even mentioned contagion. Instead, he's primarily relied on cultural objections, while downplaying immigration's economic benefits.[4]

Which makes me wonder: Has the present crisis shed any new light on our earlier disagreements? The answer: Yes on both counts.

Culturally, the crisis has shown that Americans have a lot to learn from other cultures. Our way of handling contagion has been clumsy at best. Maybe we should have learned from Singapore and South Korea, maybe we should have learned from Iceland and Sweden. What Americans definitely shouldn't do is look in the mirror and admire our wonderfully functional culture. We're not the worst on Earth, but now is a fine time to embrace a curious cosmopolitan perspective.

The economic lesson of the crisis is truly clear-cut. Since mid-March, the greatest economy in human history has been in "shutdown" or "lockdown." Our standard of living has crashed, and unemployment is near the level of the Great Depression. Why? *Because we have temporarily annulled the right of free migration within the United States.* Let me repeat that: *Our standard of living has crashed because we have temporarily annulled the right of free migration within the United States.* Americans are no longer able to work and shop where they like. The result is not a minor inconvenience, but disaster. We are suddenly stuck in a post-apocalyptic movie. I detest hyperbole. But this, my friends, is no hyperbole.

What would we think, however, if this economic shutdown had existed for all of living memory? We'd probably be content with the only life we've ever known. We only know what we're missing because – until very recently – *we had it*. And we all look forward to a future where we can restore free migration within the United States and regain its immense benefits.

What does this have to do with immigration? To quote Obi-Wan Kenobi, "More than you possibly can imagine."[5] In normal times, current immigration law keeps the whole world on permanent lockdown. While people can usually move freely within their countries of birth, governments strictly regulate international mobility. This regulation traps billions of people in unproductive backwaters of the global economy. Current policies don't just needlessly impoverish all the would-be migrants eager to build better lives for themselves. They also impoverish their billions of customers. *The secret of mass consumption is mass production.* This is the most fundamental lesson of economics. When you shut down the restaurant industry, you don't just hurt waiters and chefs; you hurt diners. When you shut down immigration, you don't just hurt immigrants; you hurt all the natives who would have purchased the fruits of immigrant labor.

Is the harm of ongoing immigration restriction really comparable to the harm of the coronavirus lockdown? Definitely.

The *highest* estimates of the fall in U.S. GDP are about 50%, and that combines the effects of the virus and the policy response.[6] Estimates of the total damage of immigration restrictions, in contrast, are *typically* around 50% of global GDP. In both cases, draconian restrictions on freedom of movement strangle production.

Even the most ardent fans of the coronavirus lockdown do not deny how much their policies have depressed our standard of living and our quality of life. Even the fans of immigration, in contrast, rarely realize how much the immigration lockdown deprives humanity year after year. How come almost everyone sees the former cost yet almost no one sees the latter? Because it's much easier for human beings to miss wonderful things they used to have than it is to miss wonderful things they've yet to experience.

Can we really compare the coronavirus lockdown to the ongoing immigration lockdown? We can and we should.

The coronavirus lockdown is only temporary and delivers a semi-plausible benefit. I'm against this lockdown. But maybe I'm wrong.

The ongoing immigration lockdown, in contrast, has gone on for about a century and delivers benefits so dubious even their fans struggle to articulate or quantify them. And when we sympathetically examine economic, fiscal, cultural, and political objections to immigration, they turn out to be either flat wrong or greatly overstated. If you want details, try my new *Open Borders: The Science and Ethics of Immigration*.[7] But here's the quick version.

1. Economic objections to immigration are totally wrong-headed. To repeat, the secret of mass consumption is mass production, and immigration restrictions strangle production

by trapping human talent in low-productivity countries. A Mexican farmer grows far more food here than he can grow back in Mexico. Not convinced? How productive would *you* be in Mexico?

2. Fiscal objections are flimsy. Despite the existence of the welfare state, boring apolitical number-crunchers conclude that even low-skilled immigrants are a net fiscal positive for natives, as long as they arrive when they're young. You don't have to take my word for it; if you like looking at numbers, try chapter 7 of the 2017 report from the National Academy of Sciences.[8]

3. Cultural objections are weak, insofar as we can even measure them. Almost all second-generation immigrants speak fluent English. Immigrants' crime rates are lower than natives'. And advanced statistical work on the effects of nations' ancestry and average IQ still imply massive gains of immigration. In a previous debate, I asked Mark Krikorian why he chooses to live in the Capital area, one of the highest-immigration regions of America. I kind of expected him to say something like, "It's hell, but I'm sacrificing my well-being so the rest of America doesn't have to endure the same fate." But if I recall correctly, he just shrugged, "It's complicated." I suppose it is complicated, but I can't understand why you would lead a political crusade against anything "complicated" when the world is still packed with stuff that's blatantly *bad*.

4. Political objections, finally, look minor at best. In the U.S., the foreign-born are, unfortunately, more socially conservative and economically liberal. But the difference is modest, even immigrants eligible to vote have low turnout, and their descendants assimilate to mainstream American political culture. It's not a big deal. Even if you disagree, why

not welcome immigrants to live and work, but not to vote?

I know this is a lot of information in a short space. I'm happy to expand on any of these topics in the Q&A. But I predictably stand by the conclusion of *Open Borders*: Immigration restriction is a solution in search of a problem. People don't really know why they want to restrict immigration; they just know that they do.

Even if my book is thoroughly wrong, though, the current crisis provides no *bonus* argument in favor of immigration restriction. Tourism – including American travel abroad – may be a problem, but we can safely admit all willing immigrants with a suitable quarantine. And such a quarantine would do little to discourage immigration, because the gains are astronomical.

Last point: If you fear a world where American citizens, in the name of disease prevention, lose their basic freedom to travel abroad, I share your fear. But when you cherish this freedom, please remember that the vast majority of the world's population has lacked this freedom for about a century. Even the world's poorest people can scrape together the money to get here; what most will never get is the government paperwork that allows them to live and work in peace. Our shutdown will end in the foreseeable future. The world's shutdown will endure until we see it for the needless cruelty it is.[9]

May 7, 2020

* * *

Notes

1. Caplan, Bryan. "Some Unpleasant Immigration Arithmetic." *EconLog*, November 19, 2012.

2. Caplan, Bryan. "Pandemics and Open Borders." *EconLog*, March 24, 2020.

3. Caplan, Bryan. "Demagoguery Explained." *EconLog*, May 3, 2014.

4. Caplan, Bryan. "Economism and Immigration." *EconLog*, May 26, 2014.

5. Caplan, Bryan. "Open Borders: Now Do You See What We're Missing?" *EconLog*, March 26, 2020.

6. Beilfuss, Lisa. "Why a 50% Drop in U.S. GDP Isn't as Bad as It Seems." *Barron's*, April 14, 2020.

7. Caplan, Bryan and Zach Weinersmith. *Open Borders: The Science and Ethics of Immigration*. First edition. New York, NY: First Second, 2019.

8. Panel on the Economic and Fiscal Consequences of Immigration, Committee on National Statistics, Division of Behavioral and Social Sciences and Education, and National Academies of Sciences, Engineering, and Medicine. *The Economic and Fiscal Consequences of Immigration*. Edited by Francine Blau and Christopher Mackie. Washington, D.C.: National Academies Press, 2017. [Since writing this, I realized that I was partially misinterpreting the NAS results. For details, see Caplan, Bryan. "Richwine on the Net Fiscal Effect of Low-Skilled Immigrants." EconLog, November 18, 2020.]

9. The Soho Forum. "Mark Krikorian vs. Bryan Caplan," May 6, 2020.

Part III

Education Without Romance

The Magic of Education

I've been in school for the last 35 years – 21 years as a student, the rest as a professor. As a result, the Real World is almost completely foreign to me. I don't know how to *do* much of anything. While I had a few menial jobs in my teens, my first-hand knowledge of the world of work beyond the ivory tower is roughly zero.

I'm not alone. Most professors' experience is almost as narrow as mine. If you want to succeed in academia, the Real World is a distraction. I have a dream job for life because I excelled in my coursework year after year, won admission to prestigious schools, and published a couple dozen articles for other professors to read. That's what it takes – and that's *all* it takes.

Considering how studiously I've ignored the Real World, you might think that the Real World would return the favor by ignoring me. But it doesn't! I've influenced the Real World careers of thousands of students. How? With grades. At the end of every semester, I test my students to see how well they understand my courses, and grade them from A to F. Other professors do the same. And remarkably, employers care about our ivory tower judgments. Students with lots of A's finish and get pleasant, high-paid jobs. Students with a lot of F's don't finish and get unpleasant, low-paid jobs. If that.

Why do employers care about grades and diplomas? The "obvious" story, to most people, is that professors teach their students skills they'll eventually use on the job. Low grades, no diploma, few skills.

This story isn't entirely wrong; literacy and numeracy are a big deal. But the "obvious" story is far from complete. Think about all the time students spend studying history, art, music, foreign languages, poetry, and mathematical proofs. What you learn in most classes is, in all honesty, useless in the vast majority of occupations. This is hardly surprising when you remember how little professors like me know about the Real World. *How can I possibly improve my students' ability to do a vast array of jobs that I don't know how to do myself?* It would be nothing short of magic. I'd have to be Merlin, Gandalf, or Dumbledore to complete the ritual:

Step 1: I open my mouth and talk about academic topics like externalities of population, or the effect of education on policy preferences.

Step 2: The students learn the material.

Step 3: Magic.

Step 4: My students become slightly better bankers, salesmen, managers, etc.

Yes, I can train graduate students to become professors. No magic there; I'm teaching them the one job I know. But what about my thousands of students who won't become economics professors? I can't teach what I don't know, and I don't know how to do the jobs they're going to have. Few professors do.

Many educators soothe their consciences by insisting that "I teach my students how to think, not what to think." But this platitude goes against a hundred years of educational psychology.[1] Education is very narrow; students learn the material you specifically teach them... if you're lucky.

Other educators claim they're teaching good work habits. But especially at the college level, this doesn't pass the laugh test. How many jobs tolerate a 50% attendance rate – or let you skate by with twelve hours of work a week?[2] School probably builds character relative to playing video games. But it's hard to see how school could build character relative to a full-time job in the Real World.

At this point, you may be thinking: If professors don't teach a lot of job skills, don't teach their students how to think, and don't instill constructive work habits, why do employers so heavily reward educational success? The best answer comes straight out of the ivory tower itself. It's called the signaling model of education – the subject of my book in progress, *The Case Against Education*.[3]

According to the signaling model, employers reward educational success because of what it shows ("signals") about the student. Good students tend to be smart, hard-working, and conformist – three crucial traits for almost any job. When a student excels in school, then, employers correctly infer that he's likely to be a good worker. What precisely did he study? What did he learn how to do? Mere details. As long as you were a good student, employers surmise that you'll quickly learn what you need to know on the job.

In the signaling story, what matters is how much education you have *compared* to competing workers. When education levels rise, employers respond with higher standards; when education levels fall, employers respond with lower standards. We're on a treadmill. If voters took this idea seriously, my close friends and I could easily lose our jobs. As a professor, it is in my interest for the public to continue to believe in the magic of education: To imagine that the ivory tower transforms student lead into worker gold.

My conscience, however, urges me to blow the whistle on the system anyway. Education is not magic. Professors can't make students better at whatever job awaits them with learned lectures on arcane topics. I'm glad I have a dream job for life. I worked hard for it. But society would be better off if taxpayers saved their money, students spent fewer years in school, and sheltered academics like me finally entered the Real World and found a real job.

November 28, 2011

* * *

Notes

1. Haskell, Robert. *Transfer of Learning: Cognition, Instruction, and Reasoning.* Educational Psychology Series. San Diego, Calif: Academic Press, 2001.
2. Caplan, Bryan. "Education: Economic vs. Academic Perspectives." *EconLog*, October 26, 2011.
3. Caplan, Bryan. *The Case against Education: Why the Education System Is a Waste of Time and Money.* Princeton, New Jersey: Princeton University Press, 2018.

Schooling Ain't Learning, But It Is Money

Lant Pritchett is enjoying justified praise for his new *The Rebirth of Education: Schooling Ain't Learning.*[1] His central thesis: schooling has exploded in the Third World, but literacy and numeracy remain wretched.

The average Haitian and Bangladeshi today have more schooling than the average Frenchman or Italian in 1960:

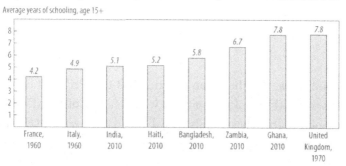

Figure 1-2. Schooling in poor countries has expanded so rapidly that the average Haitian or Bangladeshi had more years of schooling in 2010 than the average Frenchman or Italian had in 1960.

Average years of schooling, age 15+

On international literacy and numeracy tests, however, the average student in the developing world still scores far below the average student in the developed world. Gaps of one standard deviation plus are typical:

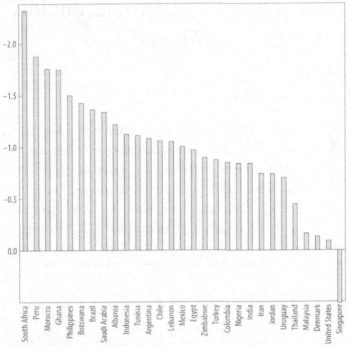

Figure 1-11. Students in most developing countries are at least an OECD student standard deviation behind the OECD level of learning.

OECD student standard deviations from 500

Solid work. But there's an amazing fact that Pritchett largely ignores in this book. Despite the woeful failure of Third World schools to teach basic skills, Third World *employers* still greatly value educational attainment. In fact, credentials pay *more* in the developing world than they pay in the developed world! Psacharopoulos and Patrinos provide a thorough survey of the evidence.[2] Quick (and conservative!) estimates say that the education premium averages 10.9% in low-income countries versus just 7.4% in high-income countries:

Table 3. The coefficient on years of schooling: mean rate of return (based on Mincer–Becker–Chiswick)

Per-capita income group	Mean per capita (US$)	Years of schooling	Coefficient (%)
High income ($9266 or more)	23,463	9.4	7.4
Low income ($755 or less)	375	7.6	10.9
Middle income (to $9265)	3025	8.2	10.7
World	9160	8.3	9.7

Pritchett's omission is striking because he's also famous for pointing out and trying to explain the fact that education is much more lucrative for individuals than nations. His leading explanations are (a) rent-seeking, and (b) signaling. My postcard version:

1. The rent-seeking story: Education successfully teaches socially wasteful job skills.

2. The signaling story: While education teaches few useful job skills, strong academic performance convinces the labor market that you've got the Right Stuff.[3]

Pritchett's latest evidence heavily tips the scales against rent-seeking. The rent-seeking story posits that Third World schools are teaching students to cleverly manipulate a corrupt, zero-sum political system. The reality, though, is that Third World schools don't even teach students how to read, write, add, or subtract – much less file a legal brief or sue a competitor.

How does the signaling model better fit the facts? Simple. Although Third World schools fail to teach literacy and numeracy, they still rank students. Indeed, Pritchett emphasizes that one of the main problems with international test scores is that weaker students tend to drop out sooner, creating an illusion of learning in the data. What Pritchett doesn't emphasize, though, is that employers can *profit* from this selection attrition by preferring more educated workers. Signaling![4]

Pritchett earnestly wants to bring literacy and numeracy to the world's poor. It's a worthy aim. But his evidence teaches us much deeper and more general lessons about the economics of education. Once you grasp how little its schools teach and how much its employers pay, the signaling story is hard to escape for the Third World. And if signaling matters enormously there, shouldn't we expect it to matter enormously everywhere?

January 26, 2014

* * *

Notes

1. Pritchett, Lant. *The Rebirth of Education: Schooling Ain't Learning.* Washington, D.C: Center for Global Development, 2013.
2. Psacharopoulos, George, and Harry Anthony Patrinos. "Returns to Investment in Education: A Further Update." *Education Economics* 12, no. 2 (August 1, 2004): 111–34.
3. Caplan, Bryan. "Why Is the National Return to Education So Low?" *EconLog*, October 31, 2012.
4. Caplan, Bryan. "The Magic of Education." *EconLog*,

November 28, 2011.

The Roots of Signaling Denial

The signaling model of education fits first-hand experience.[1] It fits the psychology of learning.[2] It explains otherwise very puzzling facts like the sheepskin effect.[3] There are few theories in economics harder to doubt. But many economists continue to do so. Empirical labor economists seem to be the worst offenders.

What gives? The charitable explanation, of course, is that the critics have fantastic counter-evidence. I've read enough of the literature to say that this simply isn't so. 40% of the economists who criticize the signaling model conflate it with ability bias.[3] Another 40% of the critics attack the straw man view that education is nothing but signaling. The remaining 20% dismiss the best evidence on implausible methodological grounds – or have standards of proof so high that no theory could possibly measure up.

If the charitable story is wrong, we have to turn to uncharitable stories. What's the *real reason* why economists reject the signaling model of education? The top candidates:

1. *Status quo bias.* Critics, like everyone else, hate to change their minds. They've disbelieved in signaling for ages, and they're not going to let anyone take their current opinion

away from them.

2. *Social pressure.* Economists feel strong social pressure to disbelieve signaling. Even though many economists think signaling is empirically important, high-status economists don't.[4] And economists are very status conscious.

3. *Provincialism.* Signaling theory comes from economics departments. But most of the best *empirics* for signaling come from psychology, sociology, and education departments. Economists don't read the research of these outsiders, and wouldn't take it seriously if they did.

4. *Liberalism.* Arrow and Stiglitz – two of the seminal figures in signaling theory – have impeccable liberal credentials. But economists still tend to see educational signaling as a free-market story. After all, the signaling model suggests that massive government subsidies to the beloved education industry could actually be exacerbating the market failure of excessive education rather than correcting the market failure of insufficient education.

5. *Education loving.* Professional economists were almost invariably good students – if not outright teacher's pets. They enjoyed their educational experience – or at least enjoyed it a lot more than most students. Education is a cherished pillar of their identity. Economists treat the signaling model as an affront to the institution they love.

6. *Panglossianism.* Many economists are Panglossian: Whatever exists, exists for a socially good reason. If massively subsidizing education is a bad idea, why does every developed country on earth do so? Even some market-leaning economists are strangely prone to this view. Some actually treat the signaling model with the same hostility as any other market failure model – even though the signaling model

strongly recommends *lower* government subsidies.

My personal judgment:

#1 isn't a big deal. Economists embrace all sorts of weird views.

#2 is a big deal for practicing labor economists. But most economists don't even realize that the consensus of labor economists largely dismisses signaling.

#3 is a big deal. Economists are as guilty of the "Not Invented Here" syndrome as anyone. Maybe more so due to our superiority complex vis-a-vis other social sciences.

#4 is tempting, but overrated. If you actually talk to economists at the AEA, you'll learn that support for massive government education subsidies is bipartisan. Mainstream Republican economists are more supportive of school choice, and less supportive of the "everyone should go to college" idea. But only hardcore libertarian economists favor significant cuts in government support for education.

#5 is a big deal. Regardless of their political views, economists were good students and love education. Even I do, in some sense.[5] Converting such economists to signaling is like persuading them to renounce their religion.

#6 is a big deal for market-leaning economists, especially the Chicago-trained. Liberal economists are never consistent Panglossians. They constantly complain even when they're in charge! But some market-leaning economists' fundamental belief isn't that markets are efficient, but that *the world* is efficient. Donald Wittman's *The Myth of Democratic Failure* is a case in point.[6]

Any explanations I'm missing? For the sake of argument, take "signaling is false" off the table.

July 10, 2013

* * *

Notes

1. Caplan, Bryan. "The Magic of Education." *EconLog*, November 28, 2011.
2. Caplan, Bryan. "Education: Economic vs. Academic Perspectives." *EconLog*, October 26, 2011.
3. Caplan, Bryan. "BAAAA! Tremble Before the Mighty Sheepskin Effect." *EconLog*, June 11, 2013.
4. Caplan, Bryan. "Economic Models of Education: A Typology for Future Reference." *EconLog*, October 30, 2012.
5. Caplan, Bryan. "I Am Not Alone: Kauffman Econ Bloggers on Educational Signaling." *EconLog*, November 2, 2011.
6. Caplan, Bryan. "How I Love Education." *EconLog*, July 18, 2012.

Abolish All Government Support of Higher Education

Why should higher education receive government support? There are two main arguments.

The first is the economic argument. Government support is allegedly economically beneficial not merely for individual students, but for society as a whole.

The second is the humanistic argument. Economic effects aside, government support is vital for the promotion of *intrinsically valuable* ideas, culture, and values.

If I merely supported spending *cuts*, I'd only need to argue that both the economic and humanistic arguments are overrated. Since I advocate full separation of college and state, however, I've got to go further. And I do.

My book, *The Case Against Education*, maintains that both the economic and humanistic arguments are deeply wrong. Economically speaking, subsidizing higher education is like subsidizing polluting industries. It's probably good these industries exist, but the free market tends to produce too much, not too little. The humanistic argument is similarly flimsy; while I share the humanists' ideals, higher education simply isn't very persuasive or transformative. The vast majority of college students arrive as philistines and leave as philistines.

146

Since Ed and I are both economists, I'll focus on the economic argument. The standard story says that college is a great place to "build human capital." Professors supposedly spend four years pouring useful job skills into their students. Why should we believe this? Because college graduates outearn high school grads by over 70%. Employers aren't stupid. If college didn't build tons of human capital, why would the labor market shower rewards on college grads?

This is a convincing story... until you remember what college professors actually teach. Sure, there are a few majors that regularly prepare their students for the world of work, like engineering and computer science. But *most* of what college students study is simply irrelevant in the labor market. In real life, how often do you use history, government, literature, foreign languages, psychology, philosophy, or higher mathematics? By and large, students can safely forget such material after the final exam, because it never comes up again as long as they live. And forget it they do.

These observations are so obvious you might wonder how anyone can deny them. Think about your own educational experience: How many thousands of hours did you spend studying foreseeably useless material? Economists' standard response is simply to double back to the labor market. If college coursework were largely irrelevant in real life, real-life employers wouldn't pay college graduates a handsome premium.

Strangely, though, there's a Nobel prize-winning economic model that explains why even the most irrelevant coursework and silliest majors can be financially rewarding. It's called *signaling*. Basic idea: Academic success is a great way to *convince* employers that you've got the Right Stuff – to show off your brains, work ethic, and sheep-like conformity. Since people with these traits are productive workers, employers happily reward people who display them – even if the display itself has nothing to do with the job.

Think about it like this: There are two distinct ways to raise the value of a diamond. The first is to give it to a gem smith to cut the diamond to perfection. The second is to give it to an appraiser to attest to its flawlessness. The first story is like human capital. The second is like signaling.

What difference does the mechanism make? For the individual student, not much. For society, however, it makes all the difference in the world. Insofar as the human capital model is right, government support for college enriches society as a whole by upgrading the skills of the workforce. Insofar as the signaling model is right, however, government support for college impoverishes society by sparking a credentialist arms race.

So which model is right – human capital or signaling? The truth is obviously a mix of both. In *The Case Against Education*, however, I argue that signaling's share of the mix exceeds half – and probably a lot more.

Why should you agree with me? For starters, look at the curriculum. Most of what we teach in college is so otherworldly that you're only likely to use it on the job if you become a college professor yourself. No sane person with a non-academic job panics because they've forgotten everything their professors taught them about history, literature, or philosophy.

Curriculum aside, you probably already tacitly agree with me. Did you bother to enroll in college or pay tuition? If all you wanted was the learning, this was a total waste, because you can unofficially take classes at virtually any college in America for free. There's just one little problem. At the end of four years of guerrilla education, you won't have the crucial signal: the diploma. Hence, unofficial education barely exists.

Suppose you could have a Princeton education without the diploma or a Princeton diploma without the education. Which would you choose? If you have to ponder, you already believe in the power of signaling. By contrast, if you were stranded on an island and had to choose between knowledge of boat-building and a boat-building degree, you wouldn't ponder. When you face the labor market, it's important to be impressive. When you face the ocean, all that matters is skill.

Signaling dominates if you look at the way college students approach their studies. They routinely seek out "easy A's" – professors who dole out strong signals in exchange for little work. Of course, you don't learn much from such professors, but who cares? After the final exam, you'll never need to know it again. Signaling likewise explains why academic cheating isn't just "cheating yourself." When you impersonate a good student, you hurt employers who hire you – and the honest students whose merits you indirectly call into question.

Academic research reinforces common sense. While economists typically measure education's annual return, scholars who look find enormous diploma or "sheepskin effects." Senior year pays far more than the earlier three years combined! This is very hard for human capital theory to explain. It makes perfect sense if college students are trying to signal their conformity by completing their degree.

Macroeconomists, similarly, have found that while individual education has a big effect on individual income, national education has only a small effect on national income. To be fair, they rarely embrace the signaling explanation; instead, they cry for better data so "we can get the right answer." But signaling cleanly explains their results: If one laborer gets more irrelevant education, he outshines the competition; but if a whole labor force gets more irrelevant education, society's time and money go down the drain. Given the small effect of education on GDP, it's hardly surprising that few researchers find that education leads to higher GDP growth. If you're still trying to figure out if your machine moves at all, you can safely conclude it's *not* a perpetual motion machine.

The most striking academic evidence for signaling, though, comes from the literature on "credential inflation." The average worker is years more educated than he used to be. How much of this is because jobs are more cognitively demanding? How much of this is because workers need more education to *get* – though not to *do* – a given job? In *The Case Against Education*, I examine all the main studies. Punchline: The evolving labor market explains only about 20% of the rise in education. The remaining 80% is credential inflation: You need college to convince today's employers to give you the same jobs your parents or grandparents got right out of high school. This is puzzling for human capital theory. Why should employers pay for B.A.s when you need only a high school education to do the job? Signaling explains it elegantly: The more degrees proliferate, the more you need to stand out.

When I present these arguments, economists rarely deny that signaling seems like a persuasive story. Instead, they usually retreat to apriori objections: Appearances notwithstanding, signaling can't be right. The most popular objection: College "passes the market test." If it were mostly signaling, someone would have figured out a cheaper signal long ago.

But this is crazy. Higher education receives hundreds of billions of dollars of taxpayer support every year – a classic sign that it *fails* the market test. There are probably plenty of socially cheaper forms of labor market signaling. But as long as the massive subsidies continue, the substitutes will remain on the fringes. The easiest way to discover good alternatives is to end government support for higher ed – and see what comes next.

At this point, you could respond, "Sure, education is mostly signaling. But the economic rewards are so great that it's *still* worth subsidizing." But signaling aside, there's far less to education's economic rewards than meets the eye.

Why? First, college graduates aren't randomly selected. Most were already high performers back in high school; if they hadn't gone to college, they probably would have been fairly successful anyway. When researchers statistically compare high school graduates to college graduates with equal pre-college ability, they almost always find the true effect of college on personal success is smaller than it seems.

Second, standard comparisons focus on people who *finish* college. But this is cheating because the college graduation rate for full-time students is about 50%. When you weigh college as an investment, this slashes the expected return.

A debate is admittedly not a great place to do arithmetic. But in *The Case Against Education*, I snap all these pieces – and many others – together. Along the way, I seriously study potentially neglected *benefits* of college: health, crime, you name it. Because confirmation bias is bad. Final result: From a social point of view, investments in college aren't just overrated; they're ruinous. Subsidizing this rat race is as economically foolish as handing out big cash prizes to the world's dirtiest polluters.

When the economic case for tax-subsidized college crumbles, even many economists suddenly discover the "finer things in life." What about the humanistic argument that college inspires love of ideas and culture – that it refines and elevates us? My quick response: Refinement and elevation would be great... if it really happened. But the actual data say that it's mostly wishful thinking. Only a minuscule fraction of college grads take a meaningful interest in ideas or culture after graduation. People who attend events like the Soho Forum for fun are really weird. That's why I love you guys!

You could agree with every word I've said so far, but respond, "Instead of abolishing government support for higher education, government should use the power of the purse to *fix* higher education." We can certainly imagine a world where colleges fill every student's mind with human capital and every student's heart with Shakespeare. Why not do that?

Simple: Defunding dysfunctional systems is almost foolproof. Fixing dysfunctional systems, in contrast, is horribly hard. As a professor, I assure you that the entire system bitterly resists even mild reforms. Most professors detest the very idea of objectively measuring the value of anything they do. They're artists! You can't deal with these people – and it's foolish to try. If someone says, "Sorry for wasting trillions of tax dollars. But we did a few good things, and we'll spend your money wisely from now on," the prudent reaction is to draw a line in the sand and say, "You're fired."

But why should we be so extreme? Why not just cut half and see if that does the trick? Pragmatically speaking, abolition is far more transparent. The scope of partial reforms is always confusing and debatable. When you separate college and state, it's clear-cut.

Since this is the Soho Forum, let me end with my principled argument for full abolition: the *presumption* of liberty. I know there's a wide range of libertarian views. In fact, there's one libertarian view per libertarian. But we should all be able to agree that the burden of proof rests on the advocates of government intervention. If politicians are going to take our money without our consent, they should at least have solid proof that the money is very well-spent. Government support for colleges does not meet that bar. Not even close.[1]

May 15, 2018

* * *

Notes

1. The Soho Forum. "Bryan Caplan vs. Edward Glaeser," May 14, 2018.

Is Education Worth It?

I s the education system really a waste of time and money, as my new book claims right on the cover?[1] This is a strange topic to debate with Eric Hanushek. Why? Because if Hanushek had absolute power to fix the education system, education might actually *be* worth every penny. Hanushek is famous for focusing on what schools teach rather than what they spend – and documenting the vast disconnect between the two. If you haven't already read his dissection of "input-based education policies," you really ought to. Hanushek, more than any other economist, has taught us that measured literacy and numeracy are socially valuable – but just making kids spend long years in well-funded schools is not.

Tragically, however, Hanushek is not our education czar. Instead, all levels of our education system are extremely wasteful and ineffective. After spending more than a decade in class and burning up over $100,000 in taxpayer money, most Americans know shockingly little. About a third of adults are barely literate or numerate. Average adult knowledge of the other standard academic requirements - history, social studies, science, foreign languages – is near-zero. The average adult with a B.A. has the knowledge base you'd intuitively expect of the average high school graduate. The average high school graduate has the knowledge base you'd intuitively expect of the average drop-out. This is the fruit of a trillion taxpayer dollars a year.

For economists, however, there's a powerful objection to this condemnation. If students really learn so little, why on earth is education so lucrative in the labor market? Why do high school grads outearn dropouts by 30%? Why do college grads outearn high school grads by 73%? Explain that! Employers want profit and they aren't dumb. They wouldn't pay exorbitant premia unless education dramatically improved worker productivity, right?

Wrong. There are TWO solid business reasons to pay extra for educated workers. One is that education teaches useful skills, *transforming* unskilled students into skilled workers. This is the standard "human capital" story. The other reason, though, is that education *certifies* useful skills, helping employers distinguish skilled workers from imposters. This is the "signaling" story. In the real world, naturally, it's a continuum. But since Hanushek is not the education czar, signaling explains most of education's financial reward.

How can we know this? We should start with the massive gap between learning and earning, combined with the fact that even the most irrelevant subjects and majors yield decent financial rewards. If human capital were the whole story, why on earth would employers care if about whether you've studied Shakespeare, Latin, or trigonometry? Think about all the classroom materials you haven't used since the final exam.

If that doesn't fully convince you, many other facts that every student knows cut in the same direction. Such as:

1. It's easy to unofficially attend college classes without enrolling or paying tuition, but almost no one bothers. Why not? Because after four years of guerilla education, there's one thing you won't have: a diploma. The central signal of our society.

2. Students' focus on grades over learning, best seen in their tireless search for "easy A's." Signaling has a simple explanation: If a professor gives you a high grade for minimal work, you get a nice seal of approval without suffering for it.

3. Students routinely cram for final exams, then calmly forget everything they learn. Signaling provides a clean explanation: Learning, then forgetting, sends a much better signal than failing.

In *The Case Against Education*, I also review multiple major bodies of academic research to help pin down the true human capital/signaling breakdown. In the end, my best estimate is that signaling explains 80% of the payoff. Key pieces of evidence:

1. Most of the payoff for school comes from graduation, not mere years of study. This is a doozy for human capital theory to explain; do schools withhold useful skills until senior year? But it makes perfect sense if graduation is a focal signal of conformity to social norms.

2. There has been massive credential inflation since 1940. The education you need to *do* a job hasn't changed much, but the education you need to *get* any given job has risen about three years. Hence, the fact that waiter, bartender, security guard, and cashier are all now common jobs for college grads.

3. Though every data set yields different estimates, the effect

of national education on national income is much smaller than the effect of personal education on personal income. How is this possible? Signaling! Give everyone more useful skills, and you enrich the whole nation. Give everyone more stickers on their foreheads, and you fritter away valuable time and tax money.

If you've been wondering, "What does signaling have to do with wasteful education?," I hope you're starting to see the link. Sure, it's useful to rank workers. But once they're ranked, prolonging the ranking game is a socially destructive rat race. When education levels skyrocket, the main result isn't good jobs for every graduate, but credential inflation: The more education the average worker has, the more education the average worker needs to be employable. And while sending fancy signals is a great way for an individual to enrich himself, it's a terrible way to enrich society.

Given Hanushek's work, I'm optimistic that he'll agree with much of what I've said. It's our remedies that starkly diverge. My primary solution for these ills is cutting education spending. In a word, *austerity*. Austerity: It's a word I love. It's a word I believe in. If Hanushek's bleak assessment of input-based education policies is right, austerity will save tons of time and money with little effect on worker skill.

Strangely, though, my opponent doesn't seem excited by this glorious free lunch. His primary solution for what ails us – correct me if I'm wrong – is to take the money we currently waste and use it to increase measured learning, especially in math and science.

I disagree on both strategic and fundamental grounds.

Strategically, spending less is easy and transparent. We

totally know how to do it. Spending more effectively, in contrast, is hard and foggy. And to make it happen, we have to trust the very education system that's spent decades ripping off taxpayers and wasting students' time.

Fundamentally, while I agree that measured learning is much more socially valuable than mere years in school, Hanushek's enormous estimates of the benefits of higher test scores are just too good to be true. In his view, higher average math and science scores not only dramatically increase our wealth, but permanently raise the economy's rate of growth. It's practically a perpetual motion machine.

But how can this be true, when the typical worker uses little math and almost no science on the job? The simplest explanation for Hanushek's results is that national test scores are misleading proxies for a much more crucial – and far less malleable – cognitive skill: intelligence. If everyone were smarter, we would all do our jobs better. But if everyone knew more science, most of us would rarely encounter an opportunity to use our extra knowledge. I use my intelligence on the job every day; but whole months go by when I don't use biology, chemistry, or physics.

In sum, if I had to hand over a trillion dollars of taxpayer money to one stellar researcher, I'd be sorely tempted to hand it to Eric Hanushek. Few educational experiments would be more fun to watch. Nevertheless, I predict the results of the experiment would be very disappointing. Entrenched interests – and legions of touchy-feely parents – would block Czar Hanushek at every turn: "Test scores? That's so narrow and boring. Let's assign more poster projects!" And even if Czar Hanushek managed to sharply boost math and science scores, I'd only expect a modest social payoff. Once we admit the massive defects of the status quo, the only remedy we can really count on is austerity.[2]

February 19, 2018

* * *

Notes

1. Caplan, Bryan. *The Case against Education: Why the Education System Is a Waste of Time and Money.* Princeton, New Jersey: Princeton University Press, 2018.
2. American Enterprise Institute. "Education Policy Debate: Is Education Worth It?," February 15, 2018.

How Lazy Is the Professoriat?

In my view, low conscientiousness is a major cause of poverty.[1] Laziness and impulsiveness lead to low marginal productivity. Sooner or later the market notices and gives you your just deserts. A smug, self-satisfied view, I know, but I'm only a messenger.

Still, I have to wonder: What would the world say if someone shined a hidden camera in my office? How hard do I really work?

I could just compare myself to other professors. But that begs the question. When I look around academia, I see lazy people everywhere. (My own impeccable department excepted, of course). Many professors virtually retire the day they get tenure. Plenty of others start even earlier. It's fairly common for tenure-track professors to "work" seven years with zero discernible output. Yet by standard measures - like grades, test scores, and educational attainment - professors are extremely successful. How do such success and such laziness coexist?

To resolve this paradox, you need to remember that laziness is a preference – and that behavior is the *reaction* of preference to environment. Before you pronounce a professor "lazy," you should ask yourself, "How would *most* people act given his situation?"

Imagine taking randomly selected people, putting them in an office, and saying, "In seven years, your peers will decide whether your research is important enough to merit a job for life. See you in seven years." That's only a slight caricature of what it's like to be a tenure-track professor. You have to decide what's worth studying. You have to figure out something original to say. And you have to actually say it despite your peers' presumptions of apathy and negativity.

I submit that, placed in this situation, the *vast majority* of people would accomplish nothing. Indeed, I bet that many people would voluntarily resign because they wouldn't know what to do with themselves. Even if, by normal standards, you have a very good work ethic, you still need someone to (a) tell you what to do, (b) clearly tell you how well you're doing, and (c) reward you before you forget why you deserve a reward. Professors, in contrast, are supposed to toil day after day on a self-defined goal, bereft of clear-cut feedback, to impress habitually apathetic and negative peers seven years in the future. Bizarre.

On a gut level, professors who don't publish appall me. Untenured professors who don't publish actually baffle me. How can they squander their once-in-a-lifetime opportunity? On reflection, though, the amazing thing about professors isn't that they accomplish so little. The amazing thing about professors is that they accomplish anything at all. They may look lazy to outside observers – and even to each other. But considering their situation, professors are amazingly industrious.

September 26, 2011

* * *

Notes

1. Caplan, Bryan. "Conscientiousness and Poverty: African Edition." *EconLog*, May 24, 2010.

How Schooling is Like Garbage Collection

Schooling has a high private financial return. But most people don't finish college; many don't even finish high school. Lots of economists are baffled by these facts, and spin complex theories to explain them.[1]

At the same time, however, I've never heard an economist grapple with a parallel puzzle: Garbage collection has a high private financial return. But most people don't even try to be garbage collectors. The explanation for this pattern is all too obvious: The high wages of garbage collectors are a compensating differential for the unpleasantness of the job.

Is this analogy ridiculous? Well, if you've always been a good student, it probably seems that way. If you're an economist – or a blog reader – you probably liked school. I bet that many of you were formerly known as "teacher's pet."

My point is that you're probably an outlier; your introspection about whether "people like school" is not to be trusted. When this happens, it's very helpful to look at representative surveys. Here's one I came across from the Bill and Melinda Gates Foundation.[2] Fun fact: The most popular reason for dropping out is sheer boredom!

Nearly half (47 percent) said a major reason for dropping out was that classes were not interesting. These young people reported being bored and disengaged from high school. Almost as many (42 percent) spent time with people who were not interested in school.

One big difference between schooling and garbage collection, admittedly, is that most drop-outs say they regret dropping out, but very few people regret not becoming garbage collectors. But I suspect that a lot of this is just social desirability bias: You're *supposed* to say that you wish you finished school, but no one expects you to say that you wish you'd become a garbageman.[3] Idly wishing you'd endured an extra year or two of excruciating boredom is one thing; actually enduring it is another. For the tens of millions of people who really hate school, the extra money just isn't worth it.

August 19, 2008

* * *

Notes

1. DeLong, Brad. "Why Aren't More People Going to College?" *Grasping Reality*, May 10, 2008.
2. Bridgeland, John, John DiIulio, and Karen Burke Morison. "The Silent Epidemic: Perspectives of High School Dropouts." *Civic Enterprises*. Civic Enterprises, March 2006.
3. Caplan, Bryan. "Self-Control and Civilization." *EconLog*, July 6, 2006.

What Incentives Does Statistical Discrimination Give?

Suppose most economists believe that "Libertarian economists can't do math," and that, on average, they are correct.[1] How does this affect libertarian economists' incentive to learn math?

You could say that this stereotype will be self-fulfilling. If everyone assumes that you can't do math, the marginal benefit of learning more math is zero, right?

Well, maybe that's right on a homework problem. But how about the real world? In the real world, there are ways of showing that you are counter-stereotypical. For example, a libertarian economist could write his dissertation on game theory under Avinash Dixit. Will people *still* assume that the libertarian economist can't do math? I think not.

In more general terms, even if people look down on the average member of your group, it's hardly clear that your *marginal* incentive to do better is worse than anyone else's. In fact, as my Dixit example illustrates, if people think your group is bad in some way, the marginal benefit of counter-stereotypical behavior is probably unusually BIG. The expected mathematical ability of a non-libertarian who writes under Dixit goes from very good to excellent. The expected mathematical ability of a libertarian who writes under Dixit goes from poor to excellent. These look like incentives for a self-*reversing* prophesy to me.

If I'm right, though, shouldn't all statistical discrimination undo itself? Sure, if groups were really the same to begin with. But they're not. Libertarians go into economics to think big thoughts, not solve equations. It would be amazing if their average mathematical ability could equal that of people who go into economics *because* they like solving equations. The result: Even though libertarians have a stronger incentive to learn math, they are still less proficient.

Overall, it seems like my example generalizes. If taxis are reluctant to pick up young, black males, then young, black males probably have an unusually *large* marginal benefit of wearing a suit. Outside of a simple-minded homework problem, statistical discrimination is a reason to try harder, not a reason to give up.

January 13, 2007

* * *

Notes

1. Caplan, Bryan. "Practicing What I Preach: How I Fight Statistical Discrimination." *EconLog*, September 28, 2005.

Regressions By Popular Demand:
Black Education Pays Extra

In my critique of Harford's chapter[1] on statistical discrimination, I wrote:

> But is it really true that the market fails to reward blacks for getting more education? Is it even true that the market rewards them less? I tested these claims using one of the world's best labor data sets, the NLSY. The results directly contradict Tim's self-fulfilling prophesy story. Blacks actually get a substantially larger return to education than non-blacks! The same goes for experience, though the result is not statistically significant. The real lesson of the data is that if you are young, gifted, and black, you should get a ton of education, because it has an exceptionally large pay-off.[2]

Here's an introduction to the kinds of regressions I ran using the NLSY. (The data comes from 1992, the most recent year on my CD-ROM that asks everyone about their annual labor income).

I start out with a simple benchmark regression of the logarithm of annual labor income on Black (=1 if the respondent is black, and 0 otherwise), AFQT (percentile on an IQ-type test), and Grade (number of years of education completed). The results are pretty standard: Blacks earn about 13% less than comparable non-blacks, and each year of education raises income by about 8%. (You can make the black-white gap completely disappear if you add family status control variables, but that's not the focus here).

Variable	Coefficient	Std. Error	t-Statistic	Prob.
C	8.41	0.07	114.40	0.00
BLACK	-0.13	0.03	-4.34	0.00
AFQT	0.01	0.00	10.87	0.00
GRADE	0.08	0.01	12.52	0.00

Note that the baseline specification assumes that blacks and non-blacks get the same payoff for each year of education. Harford's chapter predicts that blacks get less. To adjudicate between these two views, all we have to do is add Grade*Black as a control variable. If Grade*Black=0, blacks and whites get the same percentage increase in earnings from a year of education. If Grade*Black>0, education actually pays blacks more.

The results are striking:

Variable	Coefficient	Std. Error	t-Statistic	Prob.
C	8.61	0.08	105.84	0.00
BLACK	-1.09	0.17	-6.45	0.00
AFQT	0.01	0.00	11.19	0.00
GRADE	0.06	0.01	9.25	0.00
GRADE*BLACK	0.07	0.01	5.77	0.00

Yes, in this specification, education pays blacks more than *twice* as much as it pays non-blacks. At the same time, adding this control variable makes the coefficient on Black *much* more negative. The upshot is that at low levels of education, blacks earn much less than non-blacks; but at high levels of education, they earn more. This result remains even if you add a lot of other control variables, but I suspect that two regressions have already tried most readers' patience.

Incidentally, the cut-point in this equation is roughly at 15 years of education. This means that blacks with fewer than 15 years earn less than comparable non-blacks; blacks with more than 15 earn more than comparable non-blacks. (Adding more control variables pushes the cut-point down to 13 years).

If this were a journal article, I'd look for a more recent version of the NLSY, and run more robustness checks. But still, it's striking that one of the best labor data sets in the world decisively rejects the view that statistical discrimination reduces blacks' incentive to try to better their lot. Instead, the data strongly support the diametrically opposed view that acquiring education is a great way for a black worker to credibly tell employers, "No matter what you think about the average black, *I've* got the right stuff."

February 18, 2008

* * *

Notes

1. Caplan, Bryan. "The Truth Hurts: What Harford Didn't Say About Statistical Discrimination." *EconLog*, February 13, 2008.
2. Harford, Tim. *The Logic of Life: The Rational Economics of an Irrational World*. 1st ed. New York: Random House, 2008.

Progress, Academics, Streetlights, and Keys

The best argument *against* vocational education is economic change.[1] What's the point of preparing students for occupations that won't even exist by the time they finish their studies? In *Left Back*, Diane Ravitch skewers Progressive-era educators for their lack of vision:

> The surveyors had a static notion of both the individuals' capacity for development and society's needs. They did not see youngsters as people with curiosity and imagination that transcended their likely occupational role, nor could they imagine a future in which men and women, by improving their skills and knowledge, could change their occupation, indeed change society. Nor had they any sense of a dynamic society in which the nature of occupations was regularly redefined by technological change.

Well-put. Vocational educators are trying to hit a moving target. Indeed, they're trying to hit a target they have yet to see. But that's life. When you prepare for an uncertain future, it's prudent to:

- Try to make a reasonable forecast using available information
- Focus more on broadly useful skills instead of narrow specialties
- Have back-up plans
- *Expect* to periodically retrain to adjust to changing circumstances

Unless I misunderstand her, Ravitch draws a radically different conclusion. To her, a dynamic economy somehow argues for a traditional academic education focused on literature, history, science, and foreign languages. What a non sequitur. Yes, it's hard to figure out which occupation students will have in the future. How is that a reason to prepare students for occupations they almost certainly *won't* have?

The economy is changing in countless ways, but it would be amazing if literature or history saw major job growth. It's easier to imagine job growth in science and (living) foreign languages. But is the labor market really likely to reward the degree of scientific or linguistic competence the typical student can realistically attain? A B+ in high school science or foreign language* doesn't open occupational doors for you today, and probably won't in the future, either.

Before they prepare their students for the future, educators should think long and hard about what the future is likely to hold. Point taken. But economic uncertainty is no excuse for traditional academic education. Teaching Latin because you don't know whether nanotech will work is as foolish as looking for your keys under the streetlight because it's brighter there.

* In fact, voice recognition technology is getting so good that I expect employers' demand for foreign language skills to sharply fall over the next few decades.

October 12, 2011

* * *

Notes

1. Caplan, Bryan. "Misvocational Education." *EconLog*, October 7, 2011.

Leftist Lessons of The Case Against Education

Overall, reactions to *The Case Against Education* have been civil and fair.[1] While I've been heavily criticized, I've been criticized for what I actually said and believe. My main disappointment: While the *quality* of the left-wing critiques has been fine, the *quantity* is modest. Yes, I had a great conversation with Sean Illig at Vox,[2] and Steve Pearlstein has a nice write-up in the *Washington Post*.[3] And don't forget my animated podcast with center-left Michael Baranowski on *The Politics Guys*.[4] But I'd still say my un-left podcasts outnumber the left podcasts by 10:1. – and at least so far, no left-leaning think tank has invited me to speak.

This strikes me as particularly unfortunate because there are *many* results in *The Case Against Education* that leftists should appreciate. Starting with...

1. *Lots of workers – especially less-educated workers – are paid less than they're worth.* If signaling is important, there are bound to be numerous "diamonds in the rough" – good workers who are underpaid because they lack the right credentials to convince employers of their quality.

2. *Lots of workers – especially more-educated workers – are paid*

more than they're worth. Again, if signaling is important, there are bound to be lots of bad workers who are overpaid because they obtained misleadingly strong credentials.

3. *A lot of education is meaningless hoop-jumping.* Campus radicals have long accused the education system of imposing an irrelevant, backward-looking, elitist curriculum on hapless kids. I say they're right.

4. *The education market is inefficient.* In signaling models, education has negative externalities. My story, therefore, implies a serious market failure, where self-interest leads students to pursue more education than socially optimal.

5. *Locked-in Syndrome.* Due to conformity signaling, the market for education isn't just inefficient; it's *durably* inefficient.[5] The education market doesn't just fail; it *durably* fails.

6. *The government's "ban" on IQ testing is grossly exaggerated, and does next to nothing to explain employers' reliance on credentials.* While the *Griggs* case nominally imposes near-insurmountable hurdles on IQ employment testing (as well as virtually every hiring method), it is cursorily enforced.[6] Lots of U.S. employers admit they use IQ testing, and the expected legal costs of doing so are tiny.

7. *Credential inflation is rampant.* Technological change explains only a small fraction of the evolution of the modern labor market. The popular perception that workers need far more education to get the *same* jobs their parents and grandparents had is deeply true.

8. *Working your way up takes ages.* While there's good evidence that worker ability raises pay, the process takes *many* years. If you're smart but uncredentialed, even a decade of work experience isn't enough to fully catch up.

9. *In many ways, the labor market used to be better for people from poor and working-class families.* Sure, average living standards are much higher today than in 1950. But in 1950, there was *far* less stigma against high school dropouts, and very little stigma against workers who didn't go to college. Moderns who look at college graduates from poor families and see "social justice" are neglecting the troubles of the massively larger number of kids from poor families who *never* get college degrees.

10. *Forcing middle-class aspirations on everyone causes misery and failure for poor and working-class kids.* Lots of kids loathe school. They're bored out of their minds, and humiliated by teachers' endless negative feedback. Such kids disproportionately come from poor and working-class families. But since the middle- and upper-classes control the curriculum, they've stubbornly moved to a "college-for-all" approach to school – and turned vocational education into an afterthought. The result: Most poor and working-class kids endure thousands of sad hours, then leave school unprepared for either jobs or college.

I don't deny, of course, that *The Case Against Education* has plenty of right-wing lessons, too. Scoff if you must, but I try to just follow the arguments and evidence wherever they lead. My point is that there is plenty between the covers of my latest book that the left should appreciate. To all my left-wing friends, I say in all sincerity that I'd be delighted to discuss all this in depth!

April 2, 2018

* * *

Notes

1. Caplan, Bryan. *The Case against Education: Why the Education System Is a Waste of Time and Money*. Princeton, New Jersey: Princeton University Press, 2018.
2. Illing, Sean. "Public Education: Why This Economist Thinks It's Mostly Pointless." *Vox*, September 20, 2018.
3. Pearlstein, Steven. "Is College Worth It? One Professor Says No." *Washington Post*, March 9, 2018.
4. Baranowski, Michael. "Bryan Caplan on The Case Against Education." *The Politics Guys* (blog), March 21, 2018.
5. Caplan, Bryan. "Status Quo Bias and Conformity Signaling." *EconLog*, August 8, 2012.
6. Caplan, Bryan. "Why Don't Applicants Volunteer Their Test Scores?" *EconLog*, May 10, 2012.

Part IV

The Search for Success

Does Burning Your Money Make You Poor?

Does burning your money make you poor? Almost everyone responds, "Obviously." And in a sense, it *is* obvious. If you take all your money and burn it, you'll be hungry and homeless as a result. QED.

In another sense, though, burning money might not change a thing. How so? Suppose if you don't burn your money, you flush it down the toilet instead. Empirical researchers who look will detect *zero* effect of burning money on your standard of living. Why? Because your Plan B is just as impoverishing as your Plan A.

As far as I know, no researcher bothers to study the connection between burning cash and living in poverty. But researchers do study analogous issues, like: Does becoming a single mother lead to poverty? At least according to some studies, once you adjust for preexisting characteristics, women who have kids out of wedlock are no poorer than women who don't.[1]

How is this even possible? You have to think about what single moms *would have done* if they hadn't gotten pregnant. Maybe they would have just spent more time hanging out with irresponsible boyfriends and partying. If so, researchers will detect no effect of single motherhood on poverty.

There's nothing literally wrong with this result, but it is easily misinterpreted. Key point: Most people who affirm that "Single motherhood causes poverty" tacitly assume a more elaborate counter-factual. Something like: "Continuously working full-time without getting pregnant." And if that's the counter-factual, "Single motherhood causes poverty" is almost as undeniable as "Burning money makes you poor." Empirical research can and occasionally does disprove common sense. But more often empirical research just addresses a different but superficially similar question.

March 20, 2015

* * *

Notes

1. Badger, Emily. "The Relationship between Single Mothers and Poverty Is Not as Simple as It Seems." *The Washington Post*, April 10, 2014.

What Does the Success Sequence Mean?

If you live in the First World, there is a simple and highly effective formula for avoiding poverty:

1. Finish high school.
2. Get a full-time job once you finish school.
3. Get married before you have children.

Researchers call this formula the "success sequence." Ron Haskins and Isabel Sawhill got the ball rolling with their book *Creating an Opportunity Society*, calling for a change in social norms to "bring back the success sequence as the expected path for young Americans."[1] The highest-quality research on this success sequence to date probably comes from Wendy Wang and Brad Wilcox. In their *Millennial Success Sequence*, they observe:

> 97% of Millennials who follow what has been called the "success sequence"—that is, who get at least a high school degree, work, and then marry before having any children, in that order—are not poor by the time they reach their prime young adult years (ages 28-34).[2]

One common criticism is that full-time work does almost all the work of the success sequence. Even if you drop out of high school and have five kids with five different partners, you'll probably avoid poverty as long as you work full-time. Wilcox and Wang disagree:

> ...This analysis is especially relevant since some critics of the success sequence have argued that marriage does not matter once education and work status are controlled.
>
> The regression results indicate that after controlling for a range of background factors, the order of marriage and parenthood in Millennials' lives is significantly associated with their financial well-being in the prime of young adulthood. Simply put, compared with the path of having a baby first, marrying before children more than doubles young adults' odds of being in the middle or top income. Meanwhile, putting marriage first reduces the odds of young adults being in poverty by 60% (vs. having a baby first).

But even if the "work does all the work" criticism was statistically true, it misses the point: Single parenthood makes it *very* hard to work full-time.

A more agnostic criticism doubts causation. Sure, poverty *correlates* with failure to follow the success sequence. How, though, do we know that the so-called success sequence actually *causes* success? It's not like we run experiments where we randomly assign lifestyles to people. The best answer to this challenge, frankly, is that causation is obvious. "Dropping

out of school, idleness, and single parenthood make you poor"
is on par with "burning money makes you poor."[3] The demand
for further proof of the obvious is a thinly-veiled veto of
unpalatable truths.

A very different criticism, however, challenges the perceived
moral premise behind the success sequence. What is this
alleged moral premise? Something along the lines of: "Since
people can reliably escape poverty with moderately responsible behavior, the poor are largely to blame for their own
poverty, and society is not obliged to help them." Or perhaps
simply, "The success sequence shifts much of the moral blame
for poverty from broad social forces to individual behavior."
While hardly anyone explicitly uses the success sequence to
argue that we underrate the blameworthiness of the poor for
their own troubles, critics still hear this argument loud and
clear – and vociferously object.

Thus, Eve Tushnet writes:

> To me, the success sequence is an example of what
> Helen Andrews dubbed "bloodless moralism"...
>
> All bloodless moralisms conflate material success
> and virtue, presenting present successful people
> as moral exemplars. And this, like "it's better to
> have a diploma than a GED," is something virtually
> every poor American already believes: that escaping
> poverty proves your virtue and remaining poor is
> shameful.[4]

Brian Alexander similarly remarks:

> The appeal of the success sequence, then, appears

to be about more than whether it's a good idea. In a society where so much of one's prospects are determined by birth, it makes sense that narratives pushing individual responsibility—narratives that convince the well-off that they deserve what they have—take hold.[5]

Cato's Michael Tanner says much the same:

The success sequence also ignores the circumstances in which the poor make choices. Our choices result from a complex process that is influenced at each step by a variety of outside factors. We are not perfectly rational actors, carefully weighing the likely outcomes for each choice. In particular, progressives are correct to point to the impact of racism, gender-based discrimination, and economic dislocation on the decisions that the poor make in their lives. Focusing on the choices and not the underlying conditions is akin to a doctor treating only the visible symptoms without dealing with the underlying disease.[6]

Strikingly, the leading researchers of the success sequence seem to agree with the critics! Wang and Wilcox:

We do not take the view that the success sequence is simply a "pull yourselves up by your own bootstraps" strategy that individuals adopt on their own. Rather, for many, the "success sequence" does not exist in a cultural vacuum; it's inculcated by an interlocking cultural array of ideals, norms, expectations, and knowledge.*

This is a strange state of affairs. Everyone – even the original researchers – insists that the success sequence sheds little or no light on who to blame for poverty. And since I'm writing a book called *Poverty: Who To Blame*, I beg to differ.[7]

Consider this hypothetical. Suppose the success sequence discovered that people could only reliably avoid poverty by finishing a Ph.D. in engineering, working 80 hours a week, and practicing lifelong celibacy. What would be the right reaction? Something along the lines of, "Then we shouldn't blame people for their own poverty, because self-help is just too damn hard."

The underlying moral principle: You shouldn't blame people for problems they have no reasonable way to avoid. You shouldn't blame them if avoiding the problem is literally impossible; nor should you blame them if they can only avoid the problem by enduring years of abject misery.

The flip side, though, is that you *should* blame people for problems they *do* have a reasonable way to avoid. And the steps of the success sequence are eminently reasonable. This is especially clear in the U.S. American high schools have low standards, so almost any student who puts in a little effort will graduate. Outside of severe recessions, American labor markets offer ample opportunities for full-time work. And since cheap, effective contraception is available, people can easily avoid having children before they are ready to support them.

These realizations are probably the main reason why talking about the success sequence so agitates the critics. The success sequence isn't merely a powerful recipe for avoiding poverty. It is a recipe easy enough for almost any adult to understand and follow.

But can't we still blame society for failing to foster the bourgeois values necessary to actually adhere to the success sequence? Despite the popularity of this rhetorical question, my answer is an unequivocal no. In ordinary moral reasoning, virtually no one buys such attempts to shift blame for individual misdeeds to "society."

Suppose, for example, that your spouse cheats on you. When caught, he objects, "I come from a broken home, so I didn't have a good role model for fidelity, so you shouldn't blame me." Not very morally convincing, is it?

Similarly, suppose you hire a worker, and he steals from you. When you catch him, he protests, "Don't blame me. Blame racism." How do you react? Poorly, I bet.

Or imagine that your brother drinks his way into homelessness. When you tell him he has to reform if he wants your help, he denounces your "bloodless moralism." Are you still obliged to help him? Really?

Finally, imagine you're a juror on a war crimes trial. A soldier accused of murdering a dozen children says, "It was war, I'm a product of my violent circumstances." Could you in good conscience exonerate him?

So what? We should place much greater confidence in our concrete moral judgments than in grand moral theories. This is moral reasoning 101. And virtually all of our concrete moral judgments say that we should blame individuals – not "society" – for their own bad behavior. When wrong-doers point to broad social forces that influenced their behavior, the right response is, "Social forces influence us all, but that's no excuse.

You can and should have done the right thing despite your upbringing, racism, love of drink, or violent circumstances."

To be clear, I'm not saying that we should *pretend* that individuals are morally responsible for their own actions to give better incentives. What I'm saying, rather, is that individuals *really are* morally responsible for their actions. Better incentives are just icing on the cake.

This is not my eccentric opinion. As long as we stick to concrete cases, virtually everyone agrees with me. Each of my little moral vignettes is a forceful counter-example to the grand moral theory that invokes "broad social forces" to excuse wrong-doing. And retaining a grand moral theory in the face of multitudinous counter-examples is practically the definition of bad philosophy.

Does empirical research on the success sequence really show that the poor are *entirely* to blame for their own poverty? Of course not! In rich countries, following the success sequence is normally easy for able-bodied adults, but not for children or the severely handicapped. In poor countries, even able-bodied adults often find that the success sequence falls short (though this would be far less true under open borders).[8] Haitians who follow the success sequence usually remain quite poor because economic conditions in Haiti are grim. Though even there, we can properly blame Haitians who stray from the success sequence for making a bad situation worse.

Research on the success sequence clearly makes people nervous. Few modern thinkers, left or right, want to declare: "Despite numerous bad economic policies, responsible behavior is virtually a sufficient condition for avoiding poverty in the First World. And we have every right to blame individuals for the predictable consequences of their own irresponsible behavior." Yet if you combine the rather obvious empirics of the success sequence with common-sense morality, this is exactly what you will end up believing.

* To be fair, Wang and Wilcox also tell us: "But it's not just about natural endowments, social structure, and culture; agency also matters. Most men and women have the capacity to make choices, to embrace virtues or avoid vices, and to otherwise take steps that increase or decrease their odds of doing well in school, finding and keeping a job, or deciding when to marry and have children."

February 22, 2021

* * *

Notes

1. Haskins, Ron, and Isabel Sawhill. *Creating an Opportunity Society*. Washington, D.C: Brookings Institution Press, 2009.
2. Wang, Wendy, and Wilcox Bradford. "The Millenial Success Sequence: Marriage, Kids, and the 'Success Sequence' among Young Adults." AEI Institute for Family Studies, June 14, 2017.
3. Caplan, Bryan. "Does Burning Your Money Make You Poor?" *EconLog*, March 20, 2015.
4. Tushnet, Eve. "What's Wrong With the 'Success Sequence.'" *Institute for Family Studies*, April 16, 2018.
5. Alexander, Brian. "What Is the 'Success Sequence' and Why Do So Many Conservatives Like It?" *The Atlantic*,

July 31, 2018.

6. Tanner, Michael. "The Success Sequence - and What It Leaves Out." *Cato Unbound*, May 9, 2018.

7. Caplan, Bryan. "My Hayek Memorial Lecture." *EconLog*, December 24, 2019.

8. Caplan, Bryan, and Zach Weinersmith. *Open Borders: The Science and Ethics of Immigration*. First edition. New York, NY: First Second, 2019.

Income and Irresponsibility

Suppose you learn that rich and poor people get drunk equally often. Should you conclude that the poor are no more prone to irresponsible drinking than the rich?

No. You can't sensibly categorize behavior as "responsible" or "irresponsible" until you know the actors' circumstances.[1] The greater the risk your behavior will lead to dire consequences for yourself, your dependents, or bystanders, the more irresponsible your behavior. The richer you are, the easier it is to avoid or remedy such consequences – and the less likely a given action qualifies as irresponsible.

Consider these obvious cases:

1. Spending $100 on dinner. This is extremely irresponsible if you only have $105 to your name, but fine when you're a millionaire.

2. Having unprotected sex. This is irresponsible when you're unable to support a child, but fine if you're prepared for parenthood.

The same logic holds for drunkenness. Heavy drinking has well-known health and employment dangers. The poorer you are, the less able you are to cope with these dangers if they materialize – and the greater your obligation to avoid taking chances in the first place.

The upshot is that if behavior does *not* vary by income, we should conclude that the poor are *more* irresponsible than the rich. If the rich actually engage in less risky behavior than the poor, the true gap is bigger than it looks.

If you're outraged by this implication, note that family status works the same way. When a childless single courts danger, he risks his future. When a married parent courts danger, he risks not only his own future, but the future of his spouse and his kids. Think about riding a motorcycle. This could simultaneously be a reasonable trade-off for a childless single *and* a reckless gamble for a married parent. Why? Because when you're a married parent, the total downside is much more serious.

Aren't family status and income fundamentally different? Not really. Neither depends on choices alone. Opportunities and luck both play their role. The virtuous path is not to bemoan our situation, but to act responsibly in whatever situation we find ourselves.[2]

March 13, 2015

* * *

Notes

1. Caplan, Bryan. "Poverty: The Stages of Blame." *EconLog*, March 5, 2014.
2. Caplan, Bryan. "I'm Too Busy Fighting Tyranny to Feed My Family." *EconLog*, January 30, 2014.

The Prudence of the Poor

A ri Fleisher in the *WSJ*:

> Given how deep the problem of poverty is, taking even more money from one citizen and handing it to another will only diminish one while doing very little to help the other. A better and more compassionate policy to fight income inequality would be helping the poor realize that the most important decision they can make is to stay in school, get married and have children–in that order.[1]

John Cochrane demurs:

> "[H]elping the poor to realize" is pretty hopeless as a policy prescription. They poor are smart, and huge single parenthood rates do not happen because people are just too dumb to realize the consequences, which they see all around them.[2]

But why on earth should we believe that the poor are "smart"? There is overwhelming evidence that the poor have substantially below-average IQs.[3] And even without these empirics, it would be very surprising if low cognitive ability failed to sharply reduce income in high-tech societies.

Cochrane would have been on much firmer ground if he'd said, "While the poor do have below-average IQs, they have more than enough brains to see the consequences of single parenthood." If he said that, I'd agree.[4] But this revised position still neglects the possibility that people who foresee bad consequences of their behavior will *fail to exercise self-control*. As a result, they predictably make imprudent decisions when their choices have pleasant short-run effects – even if the long-run results are predictably awful.

The empirics on the poor's lack of self-control are not as abundant as the empirics on the poor's low IQ. But the empirics are out there.[5] And even if there were no empirics at all, it would be very surprising if low self-control failed to sharply reduce income in a high-tech society.

Does this undermine Cochrane's claim that "[H]elping the poor to realize" is pretty hopeless as a policy prescription"? At first glance, no. When someone has low intelligence, it's hard to make him realize stuff; when someone has low self-control, it's hard to make him *act* on what he realizes.

On further reflection, though, there are multiple ways to make people "realize." The most popular – and, I suspect, the one Cochrane dismisses – is publicly-funded nagging. An alternative route to realization, though, is simply cutting government subsidies for imprudent behavior.

Such cuts have two effects. First, cutting subsidies for imprudent behavior makes the imprudence even more blatant than it already was. Second, cutting subsidies for imprudent behavior makes the behavior's unpleasant consequences happen *sooner*, potentially deterring even the highly impulsive. As Scott Beaulier and I put it:

> What do these behavioral findings have to do with the poor? Take the case of single mothers. On the road to single motherhood, there are many points where judgmental biases plausibly play a role. At the outset, women may underestimate their probability of pregnancy from unprotected sex. After becoming pregnant, they might underestimate the difficulty of raising a child on one's own, or overestimate the ease of juggling family and career. Policies that make it easier to become a single mother may perversely lead more women to make a choice they are going to regret.
>
> A simple numerical example can illustrate the link between helping the poor and harming them. Suppose that in the absence of government assistance, the true net benefit of having a child out-of-wedlock is -$25,000, but a teenage girl with self-serving bias believes it is only -$5000. Since she still sees the net benefits as negative she chooses to wait. But suppose the government offers $10,000 in assistance to unwed mothers. Then the perceived benefits rise to $5000, the teenage girl opts to have the baby, and ex post experiences a net benefit of -$25,000 + $10,000 = -$15,000.[6]

As far as poverty policy goes, I suspect that Cochrane and I are on the same austerian page.[7] My fear is that he's discrediting the correct conclusion with implausible justifications. The

Chicago descriptive view that everyone is "smart" has little to do with the Chicago prescriptive view that government is way too big. Indeed, as Donald Wittman has shown, it's hard to argue that government is way too big *unless* you're willing to insult the intelligence of a great many people.[8] I'm happy to bite that bullet.[9] Cochrane should do the same.

January 17, 2014

* * *

Notes

1. Fleischer, Ari. "How to Fight Income Inequality: Get Married." *The Wall Street Journal*, January 12, 2014.
2. Cochrane, John. "The Grumpy Economist: Two Points on Inequality." *The Grumpy Economist*, January 13, 2014.
3. Herrnstein, Richard, and Charles Murray. *The Bell Curve: Intelligence and Class Structure in American Life.* 1st Free Press pbk. ed. New York: Simon & Schuster, 1996.
4. Caplan, Bryan. "'How Deserving Are the Poor?': My Opening Statement." *EconLog*, February 2, 2012.
5. Beaulier, Scott, and Bryan Caplan. "Behavioral Economics and Perverse Effects of the Welfare State." *Kyklos* 60, no. 4 (November 2007): 485–507.
6. Beaulier, Scott, and Bryan Caplan. "Behavioral Economics and Perverse Effects of the Welfare State." *Kyklos* 60, no. 4 (November 2007): 491.
7. Caplan, Bryan. "Austerity for Liberty." *EconLog*, September 13, 2010.
8. Caplan, Bryan. "From Friedman to Wittman: The

Transformation of Chicago Political Economy." *Econ Journal Watch* 2, no. 1 (April 2005): 1–21.

9. Caplan, Bryan. *The Myth of the Rational Voter: Why Democracies Choose Bad Policies*. Princeton: Princeton University Press, 2007.

If You Don't Like It

Suppose your boss screams all the time, has extremely bad breath, or requires all his employees to speak in a faux British accent. Even today, the law usually offers you no recourse – except, of course, for "If you don't like it, quit." Discrimination law has carved out a list of well-known exceptions to employment-at-will. But "If you don't like it, quit," remains the rule.

While researching firing aversion,[1] I came across an interesting piece by Mark Roehling showing that few American employees realize that the law affords them almost no protection against discharge.[2] Empirically, his work seems sound. But Roehling also clearly wishes that American workers had the kind of legal protection they falsely believe they already possess. Yes, he admits, employment-at-will has some academic defenders:

> Legal scholars adopting classical or neoclassical contract law perspectives argue that employment at-will is justified in that it preserves the principle of freedom of contract, promoting efficient operation of labor markets and advancing individual autonomy (e.g., Epstein, 1984).

199

But:

> The standard rejoinder to this argument is that em-
> ployees' "consent" to at-will employment is, in many
> instances, neither voluntary nor informed due to
> inequality in bargaining power between employers
> and employees and asymmetric information (i.e.,
> the lack of equal information about future risks
> and the effect of at-will disclaimers) that both tend
> to favor employers (Blades, 1967). These defects
> in the bargaining process, it asserted, cause at-will
> employment to be both inefficient and unfair.

How solid is Roehling's "standard rejoinder"? Let's start with
"inequality in bargaining power." Sounds sinister. But we
could just as easily say, "some people have more to offer than
others – and the more you have to offer, the better a deal you'll
get." Then it sounds utterly trivial.

In any case, what would the economy look like if people
could only make deals when they happened to have "equal
bargaining power"? Almost all trade would be forbidden.
Parties have equal bargaining power about as often as they
have equal heights. The beauty of the price mechanism is that
it persuades *unequals* to trade by giving parties with more to
offer a sweeter deal.

Roehling's invocation of "asymmetric information" is even
more off-target. In any standard asymmetric information
model, the effect is not to "favor" parties with more information, but to *scare off parties with less information*, leading to
fewer trades and making both sides poorer. The upshot: If the
law somehow solved the asymmetric information problem,

the result would be a big increase in labor supply – presumably making Roehling's first problem – unequal bargaining power – even worse.

Still, Roehling's intuitions are clearly widely held. My question for people who share his intuitions: Why don't the same arguments make you want to tightly regulate the dating market? With a few exceptions, modern dating markets are based on a strong version of "If you don't like it, break up." People's complaints about romantic partners are endless: "He's mean to me," "She nags me," "He's cheap," "She won't have sex before marriage," etc. Yet prior to marriage, "If you don't like it, break up," is virtually your only legal recourse.

If you take Roehling's "unequal bargaining power" or "asymmetric information" rejoinders seriously, current rules of the dating market should outrage you. Think about the inequality of bargaining power between, say, Channing Tatum and an unattractive single mom who cleans hotel rooms for a living. He has movie-star looks, magnetic personality, fabulous riches, and millions of female fans; she's ugly, poor, alone, and responsible for her child's support. As a result, he could practically dictate the terms of any relationship. Does this mean she should have some recourse beyond, "If you don't like how Channing treats you, break up"?

The same goes for asymmetric information. People keep all kinds of secrets from those they date – past relationships, current entanglements, income, philosophy, whether they'll ever commit. And again, people's ultimate legal threat against romantic partners' concealed information and dishonesty is only, "If you don't like it, break up."

You could say we have a double standard because personal relationships, unlike work relationships, are too complicated to regulate. Maybe so, but I doubt it. Work relationships are incredibly complex, too. It's almost impossible to objectively define a "bad attitude," but no one wants to employ someone who's got one. You could argue that if we regulate one aspect of unequal bargaining power in the dating market, it will just resurface elsewhere. But that holds for the labor market as well: If the law requires employers to provide health insurance, they'll obviously cut wages to compensate. The simple story works best: The apparent double standard is real. Since people resent employers, they're quick to rationalize policies that tip the scales against them – even if employees ultimately bear the cost.

"If you don't like it, quit" and "If you don't like it, break up," sound unappealing – even heartless. But in the real world, it's hard to do better. In any case, trying to "do better" is probably unjust. The fact that Channing Tatum has incredibly high value in the dating market is a flimsy excuse to restrict his freedom to date. And the fact that Peter Thiel has incredibly high value in the labor market is a flimsy excuse to restrict his freedom to hire. Instead of complaining about the stinginess of people who have lots to offer, we should celebrate the universal human right to say, "I don't want to see you anymore."

June 7, 2012

* * *

Notes

1. Caplan, Bryan. "Naming the Puppy: Firing Aversion and the Labor Market." *EconLog*, February 5, 2012.

202

2. Roehling, Mark. "The 'Good Cause Norm' in Employment Relations: Empirical Evidence and Policy Implications." *Employee Responsibilities and Rights Journal* 14, no. 2 (September 1, 2002): 91–104.

Job Search and the Laws of Wing-Walking

W hen people examine the job market, they usually see vast inequality of bargaining power. The job-seeker needs money to live; the employer, in contrast, faces only a minor inconvenience if a position remains vacant.

On reflection, this is oversimplified. Some applicants – spouses of full-time workers, children of comfortable parents, older workers with hefty nest-eggs – are quite secure even if they remain unemployed. Some employers – small business owners, marginal managers, anyone with tight deadlines for major contracts – are sweating bullets. But it's hard to entirely dismiss the normal view. If workers in search of a job really feel like, "I can take it or leave it," why do so many applicants rush to accept their first offer?

Career counselors often criticize such workers for their lack of nerve: You should have bargained harder![1] But this seems foolhardy to me. Instead, I'd advise nervous workers to heed the First Law of Wing-Walking: *Never let hold of what you've got until you've got hold of something else.*

In practical terms: Happily settle for your first tolerable job offer… but only temporarily. Once you're secure in your new position, at least keep your eyes open for a better opportunity. Something's bound to come along eventually – and when it does, you can bargain with confidence.

Better yet, virtually any job yields valuable experience and career connections. As a result, you have more than happenstance on your side. Month after month, year after year, the odds tilt more and more in your favor – especially if you strive to impress your whole social network with your professionalism.

In theory, admittedly, employers could solve this problem by offering binding long-run employment contracts: "You're desperate? Great; sign this forty-year contract." But few employers try, and even fewer succeed. Long-term labor contracts are too damn hard to enforce.

If the First Law of Wing-Walking works so well, why do so many employees feel trapped in dead-end jobs? The most obvious explanation, of course, is that they're *not* underpaid; their low productivity justifies their low wages.

This story is greatly under-rated, but I doubt it's the full explanation.[2] There are plenty of good workers who toil in obscurity. Could they refrain from job search for fear that their current employer will find out and retaliate? It's logically possible, but I've never heard of such a thing actually happening. Monitoring is too hard, and firing seasoned workers to deter others from leaving is very costly.

Why then do some good workers have such bad jobs? Probably because they ignore the Second Law of Wing-Walking*: *Once you've got something better within your grasp, grab it and move forward.* Good workers get stuck in bad jobs because they're too complacent to search for a better job, or even keep their eyes open for greener pastures. The job market is a cornucopia of opportunity. But like God, it helps those who help themselves.

* Since nothing currently googles for "Second Law of Wing-Walking," I call dibs.

August 28, 2018

* * *

Notes

1. Sweeney, Camille, and Josh Gosfield. "49% Of Job Candidates Never Negotiate An Initial Employment Offer. Do." *Fast Company*, November 11, 2013.
2. Caplan, Bryan. "Social Desirability Bias: How Psych Can Salvage Econo- Cynicism." *EconLog*, April 21, 2014.

Big Break Theory

`

People often hope for a "big break" – a large, durable improvement in their situation. An unknown actor landing a major role in a big-budget film is the classic example. But big breaks seem to be everywhere: getting your first tenure-track job, becoming the new protege of the boss, or marrying someone way too good for you.

Once we accept that big breaks are common in reality, economists' next task is to explain how they're possible in theory. The top three models:

1. *Discontinuity of the world.* The simplest story claims that opportunities are extremely discontinuous. As a result, the gap between your best option and your second-best option is often large. So when market forces change, some people predictably experience benefits that seem all out of whack with the size of the shift.

2. *Imperfect information.* A subtler story says that while *opportunities* are fairly continuous, *discovery* of opportunities is costly and haphazard. For some people, of course, the crucial missed discovery is that, given their skills, they should be grateful for what they have. For most people, however, the reality is that there are *many* better ways to spend their lives...

if only they could pinpoint them – or convince others that they're deserving.[1] Sadly, though, it takes a lifetime to uncover even a tiny fraction of your opportunities in this world.

3. *Rationing.* This story says that big breaks happen because markets don't clear. Sometimes the reason is government regulation. Think about winners of each year's Diversity Immigrant Visas: from Third World poverty to First World luxury by the luck of the draw. On a smaller scale, think about all the people praying for a rent-stabilized apartment in Manhattan – or an old-fashioned union job.

Still, the reason doesn't have to be government. Social norms impede market-clearing too.[2] Think about the hundreds of qualified applicants for every position in mortgage-backed securities or construction in 2010. Wages stayed high, but even interviews were almost impossible to find. The same goes, of course, for gender-role norms.[3] Imagine a major war leads to a low male/female ratio. If social norms don't adjust in men's favor, there will be a shortage (in the technical supply-and-demand sense) of men. Women who still manage to marry on traditional terms enjoy a big break.

How important are these three stories? I say that #1 is rarely relevant; any appearance of extreme discontinuity in the world is just a reflection of our ignorance of the world's countless intermediate possibilities. #2, in contrast, is always relevant. Even in a fairly simple society, the number of conceivable arrangements of resources is vast, and life's too short to explore more than a handful. #3, finally, varies widely in relevance. The more market-oriented and less tradition-bound a society is, the less #3 matters. But I've yet to hear of a society where #3 wasn't a big deal.

Am I too quick to dismiss #1? I think not.[4] Heart-broken youths gravitate to such stories. But everyone older and wiser wisely avers that there are lots of good fish in the sea. And if #1 isn't even true for matters of the heart, how could it be true for matters of hard-boiled business?

February 4, 2013

* * *

Notes

1. Caplan, Bryan. "Diamonds in the Rough." *EconLog*, July 6, 2011.
2. Caplan, Bryan. "Posner's Primer on Wage Rigidity." *EconLog*, January 16, 2009.
3. Caplan, Bryan. "A Critique of Wisdom." *EconLog*, December 3, 2012.
4. Caplan, Bryan. "Reply to Arnold on PSST." *EconLog*, November 15, 2011.

Business Brainwashing and Vocational Education

I'm a huge fan of child labor, also known as "vocational education."[1] Almost everyone would be better off if students in the bottom half of their class began full-time apprenticeships after elementary school. If you hate sitting still and you're old enough to work, you should probably leave school and learn a trade. The current system prepares such kids to do zero jobs; at least my proposal would prepare them to do one job. In slogan form: 1>0.[2]

David Balan, one of my three favorite liberals, leveled an interesting objection to my proposal, shared with his permission. David's concern: Expanding vocational education would intensify the already severe problem of business brainwashing. In his view, the business world is infected by narrow materialism, unquestioning conformism, and outright deception. Academic education is a vital counterbalance. School teaches us to question the status quo, to think for ourselves, and appreciate the plurality of values. David admits that some teens need to learn how to please the customer and respect their supervisors. But this worker-bee mentality can easily go too far. Expanding vocational education would make matters even worse than they already are.

My apologies to David if I'm failing his Ideological Turing Test; I'm happy to post any corrections or clarifications he provides.[3] At least as stated, though, David is proverbially straining out a gnat and swallowing a camel.

1. Due to anti-market bias, most people view business propaganda with deep cynicism. This doesn't mean that normal people have a Spock-like ability to tune out marketing. But our default response to business propaganda is a sarcastic inner, "Yea, yea, yeaaa."

2. As a result of people's deep skepticism, businesses know that they have almost no hope of changing anyone's core values. That's why most businesses appeal to basic human drives, also known as "the lowest common denominator": hedonism, lust, vanity, and greed. It's easy to blame these traits on capitalism, but evolutionary psychology says otherwise.

3. In any case, the business world suffers from a severe public goods problem. Business as a whole might benefit if businesses joined forces to inculcate pro-business attitudes. But each individual business is better off jockeying for market share, even if it hurts the image of their industry or business in general: "Let our competition worry about the health of the capitalist system."

4. Academic education does indeed instill a distinct set of values. But I see near-zero evidence that schools encourage students to "think for themselves." Even college professors who openly glorify independent thinking rarely welcome it in practice. So what values do schools really instill? From what I've seen, American schools – primary, secondary, and tertiary, public and private – push nationalism, blind worship of majority rule, and the Whig theory of history. Every

regulation the U.S. government ever adopted and every war the U.S. fought (except Vietnam and maybe Iraq II) was a Very Good Idea.

5. Academic propaganda is markedly more persuasive than business propaganda because (a) people trust kindly teachers far more than they trust greedy businessmen, and (b) governments are better at overcoming the public goods problems of indoctrination.

6. Academic propaganda is intrinsically more *dangerous* than business propaganda. Nationalism, blind worship of majority rule, and the Whig theory of history can and usually do lead to popular self-righteous support for the mistreatment of foreigners and other unpopular out-groups.[4] Yes, xenophobia, like hedonism, lust, vanity, and greed, is part of human nature. But xenophobia is much easier to manipulate, and most adults are too lazy to severely mistreat out-groups on their own initiative.

7. Reality check: Almost no one is eager to kill for his employer or favorite corporation. Millions are eager to kill for their flag and country. Business propaganda is kind of stupid, but academic propaganda is downright scary.[5]

The main shortcoming of business propaganda, in my view, is that it neglects workers in favor of consumers. Businesses try a lot harder to shape our buying habits than our work habits. Vocational education would help correct this imbalance. If C, D, and F students started apprenticeships right after elementary school, they would spend their teenage years in a peer group where hard work and a can-do attitude are the path to high status. This would work wonders for underachievers, especially macho teen males, who currently gravitate to idleness and crime.

August 2, 2013

* * *

Notes

1. Caplan, Bryan. "Misvocational Education." *EconLog*, October 7, 2011.
2. Caplan, Bryan. "1>0, and Other Thoughts on Apprenticeships." *EconLog*, May 31, 2012.
3. Caplan, Bryan. "The Ideological Turing Test." *EconLog*, June 20, 2011.
4. Caplan, Bryan. "Why Should We Restrict Immigration?" *Cato Journal* 32, no. 1 (January 1, 2012).
5. Caplan, Bryan. "Tranquility for A Dollar a Day: An Open Letter to Adbusters." *EconLog*, November 14, 2005.

The Prideful Worker Effect

Both economists and laymen often claim that unemployment statistics paint an overly rosy picture of the labor market. Why? Because they refuse to count *discouraged workers* as "unemployed." To qualify as "unemployed," you have to look for a job. But especially during recessions, many workers who genuinely want jobs abandon their search because their efforts seem hopeless.

The next step: As soon as the discouraged workers tell the government they've stopped looking, they're officially converted from "unemployed" to "out of the labor force." This problem seems unusually important during the recent recovery – the unemployment rate is falling, but so is the labor force participation rate.[1]

I have no doubt that the Discouraged Worker Effect is real and sizable. But almost no one discusses a potentially important offsetting effect. I call it the Prideful Worker Effect. Key idea: Some officially unemployed workers have unreasonably high expectations. They focus their job search on positions for which they are underqualified – and ignore lower-status but more realistic opportunities. Officially, they're "unemployed." In reality, though, we should probably consider them "out of the labor force."

Intuitively, I'm not an unemployed astronaut, because I'm not an astronaut at all. If I held out for a job as an astronaut, the statistician who codes me as "unemployed" turns my delusion into a folie a deux.

The Prideful Worker Effect, like the Discouraged Worker Effect, is a matter of degree. We could argue for hours about whether any particular individual belongs in either box. So it's no wonder that official statistics prefer bright lines, even if the bright lines are misleading. But vagueness has not prevented economists from *trying* to measure the prevalence of discouraged workers. Why not come up with some plausible measures of prideful workers, and see what we find?

December 31, 2013

* * *

Notes

1. Bureau of Labor Statistics. "Labor Force Statistics from the Current Population Survey."

Your Money or Yourself

Most people care a lot more about money than I do, but even so, almost no one wants to be married for their money. It's puzzling. You might say that since marriage is a long-term contract, people only want to be married for traits that they will keep for a long time. But that cuts against the obvious fact that people care a lot about the appearance of their spouse, even though looks generally fade long before money does.

Another possible explanation for the asymmetry is the discrete nature of the marriage contract. Right after someone marries you for your money, they no longer need you for your money, because (prenup aside) they can divorce you and grab a big chunk of your lifetime income. Maybe that's right, but even if you've got a Massey prenup, you still want to be married "for yourself," not your money.[1]

When economics fails, I usually try to supplement it with psychology. Maybe the main reason people don't want to be married for their money is that we don't believe that people *can* love someone for their money. You can feel strong attraction to someone's personality, looks, intelligence, or success, but not money per se. The catch is that once you start loving someone for one or more of these traits, you often stay in love with them after they fade. You get addicted to the pusher, rather than the drug.

Perhaps this is too much of a man's perspective. It's hard not to feel disgusted at a man who marries for money, but we judge women who do so far less harshly. And the reason, I suspect, is that men almost never fall in love with a women for her money, but some women can fall in love for a man for his money. But that doesn't sound quite right to me. Like George Costanza, "I know less about women than anyone in the world." Still, aren't women much more attracted to success than money? An average guy who inherits millions isn't interesting to women in the same way that a self-made millionaire is.

Whatever the explanation, the fact that people don't want to be married for their money explains some puzzles about the marriage market. For one thing, it explains why people prefer to marry within their social class. If you're a rich guy, you would rather marry a rich girl because you know she's not after your money. If disaster struck her family fortune the day after the wedding, you might not care at all about the financial loss, because at least you know that she married you for yourself.

An even bigger puzzle we can explain is why men don't exploit the INS marriage loophole far more than they do. By going to the world market, the typical American man could probably use the lure of citizenship and a First World standard of living to find a wife who is better-looking, younger, and less demanding than he could find in the States. Roll your eyes if you must!

But only an idiot wouldn't wonder "Maybe she's just marrying me for the green card and the green." And that's usually enough to overpower the palpable benefits of casting a wider net.

July 2, 2005

* * *

Notes

1. "Intolerable Cruelty," *Wikipedia.*

The College Premium vs. the Marriage Premium: A Case of Double Standards

For males, the college premium and the marriage premium are roughly equal. In the NLSY, for example, you earn 34% more if you're a college grad, and 44% more if you're a married male*:

Variable	Coefficient	Std. Error	t-Statistic
C	9.07	0.11	80.68
HSGRAD	0.24	0.05	4.72
COLGRAD	0.34	0.05	6.61
BLACK	-0.03	0.03	-0.87
MALE	-0.05	0.07	-0.77
EXPER	0.01	0.01	2.15
MARRIED*MALE	0.44	0.05	9.61
MARRIED*(1-MALE)	-0.10	0.04	-2.25
CHILDNUM*MALE	-0.03	0.02	-1.63
CHILDNUM*(1-MALE)	-0.20	0.02	-10.05
AFQT	0.01	0.00	9.57

When people – economists and non-economists alike – look

at the size of that college premium, they usually conclude that more people should go to college. On a personal level, they urge individuals to enroll. On a policy level, they don't just favor all the existing measures that encourage college attendance; they want government to redouble its efforts.

Funny thing, though. When people – economists and non-economists alike – look at the size of the male marriage premium, they barely respond. On a personal level, that 44% premium doesn't lead them to urge men to marry. On a policy level, the 44% premium probably wouldn't even increase opposition to the marriage tax – much less inspire support for a massive government effort to encourage men to wed. Why the discrepancy?

1. You could point out that (a) married women earn 10% *less*, and (b) more men can't marry unless more women marry. But the male marriage bonus vastly exceeds the female marriage penalty. Indeed, the net premium for a couple almost exactly equals the college premium.

2. You could object that the marriage premium is largely selection rather than treatment. But like the college premium, the real story is probably that it's a mix of both.[1]

3. You could object that men fail to marry despite the high premium because they would *hate* being married. But you can say the same about school: Students give up because they find it super boring.[2]

4. You could object that encouraging marriage restricts people's freedom, but encouraging college doesn't. But this makes no sense. If using taxes, subsidies, and regulations to make college more attractive doesn't "restrict freedom," why would using taxes, subsidies, and regulations to make marriage more attractive "restrict freedom"?

5. You could say that education has positive externalities, but marriage doesn't. But this is irrelevant, because the people pushing college are focusing on the *private* return. In any case, the externalities of marriage are far *less* debatable than the externalities of education.[3]

I could be missing something; if you think so, let me know. My considered judgment, though, is that the double standard is all too real. People should push both education and marriage – or neither.

* I interact married and number of children (CHILDNUM) with gender dummies to allow the effects of family status to vary by gender. AFQT is the NLSY's IQ measure.

January 23, 2012

* * *

Notes

1. Caplan, Bryan. "Correcting For Ability Bias By Measuring Ability." *EconLog*, January 2, 2012.
2. Caplan, Bryan. "Earth to Educators: People Hate School." *EconLog*, February 21, 2007.
3. Caplan, Bryan. "Marsh vs. A Simple, Effective Way to Avoid Poverty." *EconLog*, September 29, 2011.

9 Short Observations about the Marriage Premium

In the past, I've faulted economists for ignoring the marriage premium.[1] Last week, when Pascal-Emmanuel Gobry[2] and Megan McArdle[3] joined my fault-finding expedition, Justin Wolfers pushed back on Twitter:

> There's no credible evidence justifying the claim that the marriage wage premium is causal.

I replied:

> Justin, you don't sound very Bayesian. [and linked to this post on economists' selective agnosticism].[4]

Justin's response:

> The Bayesian reading is to confess to a prior that there's strong selection into marriage.

After reading this, reasons for Justin to rethink his position kept popping into my head. Here are the top nine:

1. No credible evidence? How about the mere fact that the marriage premium (for men) and marriage penalty (for women) persists after controlling for age, education, race, and a long list of other confounding variables?

2. "Strong selection" hardly implies zero treatment effect – and the observed male marriage premium is so large (often over 40%) that the absolute treatment effect would still be large even if 75% of the difference were due to selection.

3. After controlling for observables, do married and unmarried men really seem radically different? What unmeasured pre-existing traits of married men could conceivably lead them to earn 40% more than unmarried men?

4. Following Heckman's lead, education economists increasingly emphasize the importance of non-cognitive skills (conscientiousness, ambition, organization, etc.). Isn't it plausible that marriage would causally raise men's non-cognitive skills via expectations, praise, nagging, devotion, etc.?

5. It's easy to see the appeal of the selection story: Married people have many traits in common: willingness to commit, to defer gratification, to conform to social norms. Why then, though, do married men earn a large premium, while married women earn a modest *penalty*? Shouldn't favorable selection enhance women's earnings, too?

6. If you say, "Women de-emphasize their careers after they marry," you're appealing to a treatment effect. And if you can believe that women de-emphasize their careers as a result of marriage, why can't you believe that men emphasize their careers as a result of marriage?

7. Kids substantially reduce female earnings. Few doubt that this effect is causal: Kids don't just take time; they change priorities. If you can believe that kids change their moms'

labor market behavior, why can't you believe that spouses change each others' labor market behavior?

8. If marriage is just a piece of paper, how can it possibly cause higher or lower earnings? Because marriage is also a state of mind. Some people (like Justin Wolfers and Betsey Stevenson) can enter this state of mind by sheer act of will. But most people need formal social recognition to effect this transformation.

9. Social psychologists have produced a lot of experimental evidence that merely identifying as a member of a group can have a large effect on behavior; see e.g. the famous Robbers Cave Experiment. Why is it so hard to believe that identifying as "Husband of X" or "Wife of Y" can have such an effect? Or simply identifying as "a Husband" or "a Wife"?

Are any of these arguments – or all of them together – good enough to convince a skeptic like Justin that a substantial part of the marriage premium is causal? Probably not. But my arguments are good enough to convince reasonable skeptics that this issue deserves far more empirical attention from economists of Justin's caliber.

March 25, 2013

* * *

Notes

1. Caplan, Bryan. "The College Premium vs. the Marriage Premium: A Case of Double Standards." *EconLog*, January 23, 2012.

2. Gobry, Pascal-Emmanuel. "Finally, Economists Acknowledge That They're Biased." *Forbes*, May 18, 2013.
3. McArdle, Megan. "Why Do Economists Urge College, But Not Marriage?" *The Daily Beast*, April 21, 2017.
4. Caplan, Bryan. "Why Aren't Academic Economists Bayesians?" *EconLog*, November 15, 2009.

What Is the Male Marriage Premium?

Married men make a lot more money than single men. In the NLSY, married men make 44% extra, even after controlling for education, experience, IQ, race, and number of children.[1] How is this possible?

There are three competing economic explanations.[2] Each of the three may be partly true.

Explanation #1: Ability bias. The causal effect of marriage on male income is *smaller than it seems*. Even after adjusting for all the previously listed control variables, men with higher income are simply more likely to be married. Maybe income makes it easier to attract a spouse; maybe Puritan attitudes lead to both income and marriage. In a pure ability bias story, marriage has zero causal effect on earnings.

Explanation #2: Human capital. Marriage causally increases male income by *making men more productive workers*. Maybe marriage makes men work more hours; maybe it makes them work harder per hour; maybe it makes them control their tempers better; maybe all of these and more. In a pure human capital story, marriage actually causes men to become 44% more productive.

Explanation #3: Signaling. Marriage causally increases male income by *changing employers' beliefs about worker productivity*. As long as married men happen to be more productive, and employers can't costlessly see their productivity, employers will rationally (and profitably!) pay married men more. In a pure signaling story, marriage makes employers expect you to be 44% more productive, but has zero causal effect on productivity.

We can summarize these competing explanations with a table:

Explanation	Causal Effect on Productivity	Causal Effect on Employers' *Beliefs* About Productivity	Causal Effect on Income
Ability Bias	No	No	No
Human Capital	Yes	Yes	Yes
Signaling	No	Yes	Yes

Economists who study the male marriage premium usually conclude that much of it is causal. This paper, for example, uses shotgun weddings to isolate the causal effect of marriage on income, and finds:

> Using the statistical experiment of premarital conception as a potentially exogenous cause of marriage, about 90% of the marriage premium remains after controlling for selection.[3]

If shotgun weddings are genuinely exogenous, we can use them to measure the causal effect of marriage. But as the preceding table indicates, there are *two* competing causal stories. And they're very hard to empirically distinguish. A shotgun marriage could causally increase your earnings by improving your attitude on the job. But a shotgun marriage could just as easily causally increase your earnings by showing employers that you belong to a category of workers – married men – that typically have a good attitude. "Selection," properly interpreted, refers to ability bias alone, not (ability bias and signaling).

If that's unclear, consider the case of tattoos.[4] A facial tattoo could causally reduce your income by giving you a bad attitude; but it could just as easily (and more plausibly) causally reduce your income by showing employers that you belong to a category of workers – guys with facial tattoos – that typically have a bad attitude. A study of "shotgun tattoos" could tell you if the tattoo penalty were causal, but couldn't empirically distinguish the human capital from the signaling mechanisms.

So what is the male marriage premium? I'm still deciding, but here's my tentative opinion.

1. The shotgun wedding paper notwithstanding, I think that about half of the marriage premium stems from ability bias. Men who marry are just more conscientious, ambitious, and cooperative, and the NLSY lacks good measures of these traits. This remains true even when men have a shotgun wedding; the stand-up guys go through with the wedding, while the slackers skulk away.

2. At least in the modern American economy, the signaling channel explains no more than 10% (not 10 percentage points) of the male marriage premium. My reasoning: When employers make hiring decisions, they heavily scrutinize educational credentials, but barely notice marital status. I

can easily believe that the signaling channel was far more important in the past; when almost every man marries, the failure to marry raises a red flag. But nowadays?

My main doubt is that I know little about hiring in more traditional occupations and regions of the country. Do employers in Kansas still raise their eyebrows when they see that a 35-year-old male applicant is single? What about CBN?

3. If the male marriage premium is 50% ability bias, and less than 10% signaling, then human capital explains the rest: 40-50%. Much of this effect probably reflects longer work hours and lower unemployment. But it's quite plausible that marriage causally increases hourly productivity by 10%.

Is my breakdown correct? If not, what's the correct breakdown between ability bias, human capital, and signaling? Please show your work.

February 28, 2012

* * *

Notes

1. Caplan, Bryan. "The College Premium vs. the Marriage Premium: A Case of Double Standards." *EconLog*, January 23, 2012.

2. Caplan, Bryan. "Ability Bias vs. Signaling Again." *EconLog*, June 28, 2011.

3. Ginther, Donna, and Madeline Zavodny. "Is the Male Marriage Premium Due to Selection? The Effect of

Shotgun Weddings on the Return to Marriage." *Journal of Population Economics* 14, no. 2 (2001): 313-28.

4. Caplan, Bryan. "Tattoos and the Labor Market." *EconLog*, February 22, 2012.

What Is the Female Marriage Penalty?

arried women earn less than single women. In the NLSY, married women make 10% less, even after controlling for education, experience, IQ, race, and number of children.[1] How is this possible?

As I explained in my post on the male marriage premium, there are three competing economic explanations, each of which may be partly true: Ability bias, human capital, and signaling.[2] What is the breakdown for the female marriage penalty? My tentative opinion:

1. Ability bias goes in the "wrong" direction. Married women are, on average, more conscientious, ambitious, and cooperative than single women – and were so long before their weddings. And at least in the modern world, high income makes it *easier* for women to find a spouse. Income matters less for women than it does for men in the modern mating market, but female income is usually still a plus. And even if income has little direct effect on women's perceived desirability, higher income indirectly puts women into close contact with marriageable men. Adjusting for ability bias, I think the true marriage penalty for women is roughly 20%.

2. Human capital explains about 10 percentage points of the marriage penalty. Even ignoring children, marriage causally reduces women's focus on their careers. Once they're married, women want more work-life balance. Some even reallocate their energy from promoting their own careers to promoting their husbands' careers.

3. Signaling explains the remaining 10 percentage points of the marriage penalty. Several commentators pointed out the fact that it's illegal to ask job applicants about their marital status. But people aren't legal robots. Interviewers frequently ask illegal questions about applicants' personal lives, and applicants often *volunteer* their personal information just to make polite conversation. When employers learn that a woman is married, they assume – correctly on average – that she will be slightly less focused on her job than an otherwise identical single woman. No matter what the law says, employers have a strong temptation to factor this information into their hiring and promotion decisions.

In traditional societies, ability bias was probably close to zero: When almost everyone marries, there's little pre-existing difference between the conscientiousness, ambition, and cooperativeness of married and single women. The human capital and signaling effects, in contrast, probably used to be much stronger. Many women – including my maternal grandmother – simply quit their jobs right after they married. Even married women who kept their jobs typically made homemaking their top priority. As you'd expect, the employers of yesteryear responded with a strong presumption against married women. Remember: Signaling is just a special case of statistical discrimination.[3]

Final thought: If the marriage-class correlation continues to increase, future employers might actually start to see female marriage as a *positive* signal.[4] Ceteris paribus, marriage will still predict a stronger desire for work-life balance; but marriage will also predict all the professional class traits that Murray discusses in *Coming Apart*.[5]

Is my breakdown for the female marriage penalty correct? If not, what's the correct breakdown between ability bias, human capital, and signaling? Please show your work.

February 29, 2012

* * *

Notes

1. Caplan, Bryan. "The College Premium vs. the Marriage Premium: A Case of Double Standards." *EconLog*, January 23, 2012.
2. Caplan, Bryan. "What Is the Male Marriage Premium?" *EconLog*, February 28, 2012.
3. Caplan, Bryan. "Educational Signaling and Statistical Discrimination." *EconLog*, September 26, 2010.
4. Caplan, Bryan. "My Two Favorite Graphs From Coming Apart." *EconLog*, February 3, 2012.
5. Caplan, Bryan. "An Optimist's Take on Charles Murray's Coming Apart." *EconLog*, January 17, 2012.

A Coupon for Kids

I magine I offer you a coupon for "CHOCOLATE – 25% off!" and you respond…

> You fail to consider that chocolate is fattening! Also, it can kill dogs. And it's linked to acne. Furthermore, many people are diabetic. And lots of people are too poor to buy chocolate even if it's 25% off. I also have to tell you that chocolate melts. Sometimes it makes your hands sticky. And when your hands are covered with melted chocolate, you might get ugly stains on your clothes. And dry cleaning costs money.

I trust you'll agree that this is a bizarre reaction to a chocolate coupon. Reasonable people will save their breath and do one of the following:

a. Take the coupon, buy as much chocolate as they originally planned, and enjoy the extra consumer surplus.[1]

b. Take the coupon, buy *more* chocolate than they originally planned, and enjoy the extra consumer surplus.

c. Discard the coupon.

But after my *Selfish Reasons to Have More Kids* argued that parents could safely curtail many of the unpleasant features of child-rearing, critics often responded...[2]

> You fail to consider that kids cost money! Also, pregnancy is sometimes dangerous. And moms have to do most of the work. Lots of people just don't find parenting appealing. Many people can't afford to have any more kids. And it's hard to travel if you have kids. Also, kids nowadays aren't much help with the chores, like they were back when we were farmers. And once your kids start going to school, they'll probably bring home some contagious diseases.

While the critics naturally think they're making telling points against my thesis, they're not. All I'm offering is a coupon for kids – a way to get the same kids with less pain and expense. So even if all the critics' "objections" are true, reasonable people will save their breath and do one of the following:

a. Take the coupon, have as many kids as they originally planned, and enjoy the extra consumer surplus.

b. Take the coupon, have *more* kids than they originally planned, and enjoy the extra consumer surplus.

c. Discard the coupon.

The story changes, admittedly, if the complaints were not just true, but *weighty and surprising.* If I offered you a chocolate coupon, and you accurately responded, "Haven't you heard that chocolate is the sole cause of cancer?!," then I should definitely reconsider my marketing campaign. Analogously, if I offered you a kids coupon, and you accurately responded, "Haven't you heard that kids are the sole cause of cancer?!," then I should definitely reconsider my natalist cheerleading.

Otherwise, however, save your breath. You can't credibly counter a coupon with a long list of familiar drawbacks of the discounted product.

October 16, 2019

* * *

Notes

1. Henderson, David. "Taking Consumer Surplus Seriously." *EconLog*, January 31, 2011.
2. Caplan, Bryan. *Selfish Reasons to Have More Kids Why Being a Great Parent Is Less Work and More Fun than You Think.* New York, N.Y: Basic Books, a member of the Perseus Books Group, 2012.

Ballparking the Marital Return to College

hen education correlates with a good outcome, labor economists are usually eager to publicize the fact. There is, however, one glaring exception. Labor economists rarely announce that the well-educated are more likely to marry a well-educated spouse – and capture a big chunk of the financial benefits of their partner's transcript.

The most obvious explanation for this omission is that the spousal education gradient is weak. But the opposite is true. Here's a revealing table from Schwartz and Mare's "Trends in Educational Assortative Marriage from 1940 to 2003."[1]

Wife's Years of Schooling	Husband's Years of Schooling					
	< 10	10–11	12	13–15	≥ 16	Total
2000						
< 10	3.47	0.60	1.42	0.52	0.16	6.17
10–11	0.68	1.01	1.79	0.65	0.13	4.26
12	1.80	2.02	15.54	7.33	2.41	29.10
13–15	0.76	1.06	9.26	14.91	6.98	32.97
≥ 16	0.17	0.18	2.80	6.33	18.02	27.50
Total	6.88	4.87	30.81	29.74	27.70	100.00
						$N = 220,209$

Assume you're going to marry *someone*. Then if you only have a high school diploma, your probability of marrying a college grad is about 9% for both men and women. With a 4-year college degree, in contrast, your probability of marrying a college grad is roughly 65%. Quite a difference.

Of course, this pattern probably isn't entirely causal.[2] But a large causal effect is highly plausible. Indeed, there are two credible causal channels: convenience and compatibility. Convenience: If you're a college grad, you're more likely to meet fellow college grads. Compatibility: If you're a college grad, you're more likely to hit it off with whatever college grads you happen to meet.

Now suppose that only half of the raw probability difference is causal. This still means that if you finish college, you're a full 28 percentage points ([65-9]*.5) more likely to marry a college grad than a high school grad. You could even say that the average college grad who plans to eventually marry can expect to enjoy the financial benefits of 1.28 sheepskins, rather than just one.[3] As long as the gender earnings gap continues, this marital return is larger for women than for men. But given modern women's high employment rates, the marital return is clearly a big deal for men, too.

Why is the marital return so rarely discussed by either economists or laymen? Probably because talking about the marital return is self-defeating. The more you talk about it, the more you sound like a gold-digger – and the more you sound like a gold-digger, the less marriageable you become![4] The thoughtful response to the evidence, though, is neither denial nor gold-digging. Instead, the evidence underscores an age-old adage: Don't marry for money; go where the rich people are and marry for love.

February 18, 2014

* * *

Notes

1. Schwartz, Christine, and Robert Mare. "Trends in Educational Assortative Marriage from 1940 to 2003." *Demography* 42, no. 4 (November 1, 2005): 621–46.
2. Caplan, Bryan. "Economic Models of Education: A Typology for Future Reference." *EconLog*, October 30, 2012.
3. Caplan, Bryan. "BAAAA! Tremble Before the Mighty Sheepskin Effect." *EconLog*, June 11, 2013.
4. Caplan, Bryan. "Your Money or Yourself." *EconLog*, July 2, 2005.

Supply, Demand, and the Rise of the Man-Child

C onsider a traditional society where all the men sell their labor and all the women keep house. You might think there's only one market, but there are actually two: The labor market and the *mating* market. Men use their wages to supplement their masculine charms (if any) when they woo. In the labor market, the compensation that employers offer workers adjusts to balance the supply and demand for labor. In the mating market, the quality of life that men offer women adjusts to balance the supply and demand for women.*

Note well: Much more than money matters in *both* markets. When men consider an employment offer, or women consider a marriage proposal, both men and women weigh intrinsic satisfaction against material reward. Still, money does matter. If there's a high male/female imbalance, women can end up spending most of the money despite the fact that they've never received a paycheck.

Question: What happens in this model when the demand for (exclusively male) labor goes up? Wages rise, of course. But so does demand for women – and women's quality of life. This might simply mean that women enjoy higher material consumption. But it could just as easily mean that women get more leisure, better birthday presents, or a big church wedding. When demand for women goes up, men who refuse to somehow match the new market price end up alone.

No doubt this model oversimplifies. But it's hard to deny that it's roughly true. When a guy gets a big raise, his wife gets a new kitchen. When a guy gets fired, his wife goes hungry too. The link between the labor market and the mating market is the best example of "trickle-down economics" around.

Next question: What happens if we move this model into the modern world? Specifically, what happens in the mating market when women start earning money of their own? The obvious answer is just to flip the initial model around. If higher wages for men lead to higher quality of life for *women*, we'd expect higher wages for women to lead to higher quality of life for *men*. And what do most men see as a "higher quality of life"? Among other things: Less commitment, lower maturity, and lower expectations of financial support. In short, the chance to be a man-child.

Funny thing: If Kay Hymowitz's description of modern malehood in *Manning Up* is even vaguely accurate, this is exactly what we're seeing.[1] Women are more economically successful, but increasingly dissatisfied with male behavior. Men are less economically successful, but pay a surprisingly small price in the mating market. There's no big puzzle here. A simple supply-and-demand story, with no mention of "feminism" or "family values," fits the facts rather well.

A sophisticated supply-and-demand story can do even better. When women have zero labor income, you'd expect them to care *a lot* about men's income. They might even marry men they loathe to get a roof over their heads. As women's income rises, however, women can afford to focus more on men's non-pecuniary traits.

The upshot: Women's demand for men isn't just higher than ever; the composition of their demand has changed. Income and income potential still matter. But women now focus more on looks, machismo, coolness, and other "alpha" traits. Holding charisma constant, working harder just doesn't attract women the way it used to. The result: Less desirable men often give up on women altogether – further tilting the effective male/female ratio in favor of the remaining men. And both kinds of men act like boys: The less desirable men have little to lose, and the more desirable men can get away with it.

To be fair, I've never dated anyone other than my wife. I could be missing something. If so, please enlighten me.

* Note: Since this is a barter market, we could just as easily say that "the quality of life that women offer men adjusts to balance the supply of men with the demand for men."

August 17, 2011

* * *

Notes

1. Hymowitz, Kay. "What's Happening to Men?" *Cato Unbound*, August 8, 2011.; Hymowitz, Kay. *Manning up: How the Rise of Women Has Turned Men into Boys*. New York: Basic Books, 2011.

Fun Facts About Population Projections; or, Are People Like CDs?

Tyler Cowen already blogged the best sentences from this excellent piece on population decline.[1] So I've decided to supply a complement: A brief critique of U.N. population projections.

Ben Wattenberg explains that the U.N.'s *World Population Prospects* gives four basic projections: High, Medium, and Low, plus the Constant-Fertility Variant.[2]

The Constant-Fertility Variant mechanically assumes that fertility rates will remain right where they are. If you're at 1.1 kids per woman, it assumes that you'll always have 1.1 kids per woman.

The other approaches do something quite different: With a few provisos, they assume that countries' Total Fertility Rates (TFRs) will asymptote to a specific rate. In the Medium scenario, the rate is 1.85 children per woman (it used to be the "replacement rate" of 2.1). If this sounds weird, it is. As Wattenberg explains:

> Until the publication of the 2002 data, the UNPD "Medium" scenario took every modern nation with a TFR below 2.1 children per woman and by statistical

fiat sloped it upward toward 2.1 by 2050. Nations above the replacement rate were sloped downward to 2.1.

Now the UN projects that TFR will fall to 1.85. Recall that every single developed nation – all of Europe, Japan, the United States, Canada, Australia – is currently in subreplacement status, and almost all of them have been there for decades. Yet for the most modern countries the new UN projections will raise the TFR for the next fifty year cycle.

In other words:

> [F]or nations with low TFRs, this does not mean a decrease in fertility, but rather a large increase. Thus the current German TFR is 1.35. Using the new level of 1.85 means going up by half a child per woman, which is quite substantial. As we shall see, there is no evidence that such an increase is occurring.

The High and Low projections basically use the same methodology as the Medium, but asymptote TFRs to different numbers: the High assumes TFR will go to 2.35 children per woman; the Low assumes it will go to 1.35 children per woman. Thus, for many countries like Russia, Japan, China, and Italy, even the Low projection actually predicts a reversal of a decades-long fertility decline.

To get some perspective, suppose that you're trying to predict CD sales in the developed world in 2050. You could assume that sales per person will continue at their current rate. That's like the Constant-Fertility Variant. You could assume

244

that sales per person will asymptote to a level somewhat above the current rate. That's like the Medium Fertility Variant. You could assume that sales per person will asymptote to a level far above the current rate. That's like the High Fertility Variant. And you could assume that sales per person will asymptote to a level somewhat below the current rate – even though large segments of the market are already well below that rate. That's like the Low Fertility Variant.

Now notice: The most obvious projection – one in which the decline in CD purchases *continues* – is conspicuously absent! And at least for CDs, isn't that the most reasonable projection? CD sales per person will fall to near-zero, and the world stock of CDs will slowly do the same.

Are people like CDs? At least for the near-term, there's every reason to think so. If fertility has been declining for decades, it's strange to assume that fertility coincidentally bottomed out yesterday. So Constant-Fertility Projections are actually probably on the high side.

In the longer-run, though, evolution will almost surely save us. If the average woman has one child, population size shrinks by 50% per generation. But if 10% of women have three kids, and if family size (like virtually every trait) is partly heritable, the proportion of the population that wants 3 kids will exceed 50% in a few generations. In a century or two, the desolate villages of Italy will be reclaimed by the descendants of those of us who think that life is a chain letter worth continuing.

June 29, 2008

* * *

Notes

1. Cowen, Tyler. "What Determines Fertility?" *Marginal Revolution* (blog), June 29, 2008.; Shorto, Russell. "No Babies?" *The New York Times,* June 29, 2008.
2. Wattenberg, Ben. *Fewer: How the New Demography of Depopulation Will Shape Our Future.* Chicago: Ivan R. Dee, 2004.

The Weird Reason to Have More Kids

Think of a trait that brings people together. It could be jokiness, religiosity, libertarianism, love of books, or fascination with role-playing games – or seriousness, impiety, statism, hatred of books, or contempt for role-playing games. Take your pick.

Now suppose that the parent-child correlation on the trait you picked is exactly zero. Then no matter what you're like, you should expect your kids to be at the 50th percentile. If you're normal, that's a pretty good deal; at least on average, your kids will be just like you. But the weirder you are, the less your kids will typically resemble you. Even if you're at the 95th, 99th, or 99.99th percentile, you can expect your kids to be perfectly average. In a world of zero parent-child correlation, weird people have little in common with their children.

In the real world, of course, parent-child correlations almost always exceed zero, and are often substantial. This doesn't boost the similarity between normal people and their children; no matter what the parent-child correlation is, parents at the 50th percentile typically have children at the 50th percentile. But a positive parent-child correlation *does* boost the similarity between weirdos and their children – and the weirder you are, the bigger the boost. Take a look:

		Parent-Child Correlation			
		$r=0$		$r=.5$	
	You	Stranger	Child	Stranger	Child
Percentile/	50th	50th	50th	50th	50th
Expected	95th	50th	50th	50th	80th
Percentile	99.99th	50th	50th	50th	95th

Notice that regardless of the value of r, normal people can expect to be like their kids. But that's not saying much, because normal people can expect to be like *any random person they meet!* The story's very different for weirdos. By definition, weirdos never have much in common with random strangers. With a zero parent-child correlation, weirdos will feel equally alienated from their children. As the parent-child correlation rises, however, weirdos' incompatibility with strangers stays the same, but their expected compatibility with their children gets stronger and stronger.

Now let's look at these facts like a mad economist. There are two ways to surround yourself with people like you. One is to meet them; the other is to *make* them. If you're average, meeting people like yourself is easy; people like you are everywhere. If you're weird, though, meeting people like yourself is hard; people like you are few and far between. But fortunately, as the parent-child correlation rises, weirdos' odds of *making* people like themselves get better and better. This is especially true if the parent-child correlation largely reflects nature rather than nurture, because you won't have to ride your kids to emulate you; they'll do it on their own initiative.[1]

You might object that meeting like-minded friends is always

easier than making like-minded children, no matter how high the parent-child correlation gets. If you're only looking for casual relationships, that's probably true. But if you're looking for deep, time-intensive, life-long connection, blood really is thicker than water.

The lesson: As your weirdness increases, so does your incentive to have kids. If you like football and *American Idol*, you're never really alone. You don't need to build a Xanadu for yourself. But if you're a lonely misfit, oddball, freak, or weirdo, then find a like-minded spouse and make new life together. Let the normals laugh at you. You'll have each other.

December 2, 2010

* * *

Notes

1. Caplan, Bryan. "The Breeder's Cup." *The Wall Street Journal*, June 19, 2010.

Made in the USA
Coppell, TX
02 February 2024

28504853R00144